Start Smart

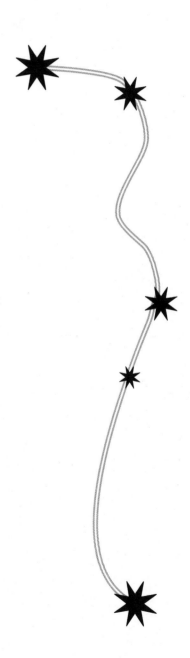

Other Gryphon House books by Pam Schiller

The Values Book, with Tamera Bryant

The Complete Resource Book, with Kay Hastings

Where Is Thumbkin? with Thomas Moore

The Instant Curriculum, with Joan Rossano

Start Smart!

Building Brain
Power in
the Early
Years

Pam Schiller

gryphon house
Beltsville, Maryland

Dedication

To my mother, Dorothy Byrne, who, like so many other mothers, used her maternal intuition to provide my brothers and me a "smart start" long before the research was there to guide her.

and

To Kathy Charner, my friend and editor, who is one of a kind in both categories.

Copyright © 1999 Pam Schiller
Published by Gryphon House, Inc.
10726 Tucker Street, Beltsville MD 20705

Visit us on the web at www.gryphonhouse.com

Text illustrations by Cheryl Kirk Noll

Library of Congress Cataloging-in-Publication Data

Schiller, Pamela Byrne.
      Start smart! : building brain power in the early years / Pam
   Schiller.
          p. cm.
       Includes bibliographical references and index.
       ISBN 0-87659-201-9
       1. Ability in children. 2. Intellect—Problems, exercises, etc.
   3. Learning, Psychology of—Problems, exercises, etc. 4. Child
   psychology. I. Title.
   BF723.A25S35 1999
   649′.123—dc21   99-17335
                                                              CIP

Table of Contents

Introduction

When old ideas, assumptions, and theories converge with new ideas, needs, insights, and technologies, we evolve as a species and move a step forward in our thinking. With the release of the brain development research, we now have access to exciting new information that enables us to offer children the best possible foundation for learning. *Start Smart: Building Brain Power in the Early Years* is filled with practical, easy-to-do ideas to apply this brain research every day.

The human brain is the most fascinating three pounds of matter on this planet, maybe even in the universe. Although often compared to a computer, it is far more complex and far more capable. In fact, the human brain takes in and organizes more information in a day than a computer is capable of processing in years. It is estimated that the human brain receives between 35,000 and 40,000 bits of information per second. Of course, much of this information is screened out or we would blow the computer equivalent of a fuse.

The human brain is capable of imagining and creating the spaceship that took us to the moon, the Alaskan pipeline, laser surgery, baseball, the automobile, the computer, Mozart's "Requiem Mass," Leonardo da Vinci's Mona Lisa, electricity, spaghetti, and playdough—all of this from an organ that is about the size of a grapefruit.

Long before birth the brain is building connections for everything from our breathing and sight to our abilities to speak, think, and reason. Although genetically the structure is in place, it will be up to the environment to strengthen and "grow" the pathways.

Start Smart: Building Brain Power in the Early Years focuses on the key findings of brain research, exploring how and when we can strengthen brain connections.

Key Findings on Brain Development

When current brain research is condensed what emerges are simple, easy-to-understand findings that, for the most part, reinforce what we know intuitively. The following is a list of the most relevant findings:

✳ Brain development is contingent upon a complex interplay between genes and environment. There is no longer the debate between whether our learning is more dependent upon nature or nurture. It is clear from the research that nature lays down a complex system of brain circuitry, but how that circuitry is "wired" is dependent upon external forces such as nutrition, surroundings, and stimulation.

✳ Early experiences contribute significantly to the structure of the brain and its capacities. The quality, quantity, and consistency of stimulation will determine to a large extent the number of brain synapses that are formed and how those connections will function. This is true for both cognitive and emotional development, and the effect is lifelong.

✳ Early interactions, how we relate and respond, directly affect the way the brain is "wired." Children learn in the context of important relationships. Brain cell connections are established as the growing child experiences the surrounding world and forms attachments to parents, family members, and caregivers. Warm, responsive care appears to have a protective biological function, helping the child weather ordinary stresses and prepare for the adverse effects of later stress or trauma. Nonresponsive care, absence of care, drug abuse, and trauma can all have an adverse effect on the child's emotional well-being.

✳ Brain development is non-linear. Learning continues across the life cycle; however, there are windows of opportunity during which the brain is particularly efficient at specific types of learning. Certain critical periods are conducive to developing specific skills. For example, children are most receptive to second-language learning from birth to ten. Children are particularly in tune with music between the ages of three and ten. Brain development is not a step-by-step process; it is more like a spiral with waves or windows of opportunity.

WINDOWS OF OPPORTUNITY			
WINDOW FOR	OPTIMAL WINDOW	NEXT BEST OPPORTUNITY	FURTHER REWIRING POSSIBLE
EMOTIONAL INTELLIGENCE	0-24 MOS.	2-5 YEARS	ANY AGE
MOTOR DEVELOPMENT	0-24 MOS.	2-5 YEARS	DECREASES WITH AGE
VISION	0-2 YEARS	2-5 YEARS	
EARLY SOUNDS	4-8 MOS.	8 MOS.-5 YEARS	ANY AGE
MUSIC	0-36 MOS.	3-10 YEARS	ANY AGE
THINKING SKILLS	0-48 MOS.	4-10 YEARS	ANY AGE
SECOND LANGUAGE ACQUISITION*	5-10 YEARS		ANY AGE

✳   Windows of opportunity are difficult to verify because results from numerous studies differ slightly. The windows in this chart are based on most frequently quoted data. The Optimal Window refers to when connections are developing at the most rapid rate, Next Best Opportunity refers to the strengthening of wiring, and Rewiring refers to the ability to make adaptations to existing wiring.

*Researchers have varying opinions regarding second language acquisition. Language is easy for children 0-5 to acquire and if children hear two languages during this time they will be able to acquire both languages and will speak both without dialect or accent. However, several researchers believe that children are better off mastering their native language before being introduced to a second language. Middle-of-the-roaders suggest offering children 0-5 years of age a 50-word vocabulary of a second language and then formal instruction between the ages of 5-10.

✷ Children are biologically prepared to learn. The brain of a three-year-old is two-and-a-half times more active than that of an adult. Children's brains have more synapses and the density of synapses remains high throughout the first ten years of life.

What Is Neuroscience?

Neuroscience research studies how the brain works. Until recently, information about the brain could only be obtained through animal studies and human autopsies. In the last decade, technological advances have allowed scientists to study the brains of living people non-invasively. We have moved from an unsophisticated model that suggested the head (brain) was responsible for our thinking and the body was responsible for everything else, to the understanding that our brain is responsible for our actions and emotions as well as our thoughts.

Using new tools—Ultrasound, CAT, MRI, PET, and EEG—scientists can study brain function, structure, and energy. The information gained through these tools has changed forever the way we view the human capacity for learning. We have broadened our perspective from a psychological base of understanding (dependent upon researchers like Piaget, Skinner, and Maslow) to one that includes a biological (science-driven) base of understanding. The combination of psychology and biology has provided us with strong data regarding how children and adults access and remember information and has also given us a new way to view intelligence.

Neural Networks

Our brain is made up of tens of millions of basic neural networks that function simultaneously and in interconnected combinations. According to Robert Sylwester (1995), if you observe a red ball rolling along a table, your brain processes the color, shape, movement, and location of the ball in four separate brain areas. Despite the debates about left and right hemispheres and special areas of the brain related to multiple intelligences, the brain functions as an integrated whole and is responsible for all of our actions, emotions, and thoughts. Indications are that we have from birth to approximately age ten to help children develop the "wiring" of the brain. The more one reads about brain research, the more it becomes evident that the key to our intelligence is the recognition of patterns and relationships in all that we experience. Strengthening a child's neural networks then becomes a job of helping develop an awareness of patterns and relationships, and helping make connections between those patterns and relationships to new information.

Brain Functions

Our brain is constantly collecting information from the environment—an average of about 40,000 stimuli per second. About ninety-five percent of this information comes to us through vision, touch, and hearing. All of this information enters our short-term memory at an unconscious level. Since it is impossible for the brain to attend to this many pieces of information at one time, it begins a screening process, seeking out what is relevant and registering only the information that matches an individual's experiences.

The filtered information is passed on to our working memory (still short-term). It is here that we focus and give our conscious attention to the information for the first time. It is here that we attempt to make sense and meaning of it. If we are able to connect the new information with existing information (if it makes sense and has meaning), it will be stored in our long-term memory.

Memory refers to the process by which we retain mental impressions or knowledge and skills that we have learned. The brain has virtually an unlimited capacity to store information. When the brain encounters new learning it goes through both physical and chemical changes. Neural networks are formed and reinforced in the process.

Retention refers to the process whereby long-term memory preserves learning in such a way that it can locate, identify, and retrieve it accurately in the future.

Using this Book

There are going to be misinterpretations of the neuroscience information. They are already beginning to surface in television commercials and magazine advertisements. You see and hear slogans about products that claim to increase children's brain power. Families are rushing out to buy baby flashcards, enrolling very young children in music lessons, or wondering if they should reorganize their finances to allow one parent to stay at home. This book was written to use the brain research to build a foundation for future learning, not to encourage early learning. Children still need what they have always needed— warm, loving, and responsive parents and caregivers; an interesting and safe environment to explore; children to play with; and healthy food and good medical care. The current research helps us give them what they need at a young age so that they will develop the greatest capacity for learning.

We must all be careful not to make generalizations or to over-simplify the information. For the most part medical research is validating what we have all known. The validation of this information and the addition of continued research will help us prepare young children for optimum lifelong learning.

Start Smart: Building Brain Power in the Early Years is a collection of activities that appropriately apply the brain research information to everyday experiences. Beneath the umbrella of the key findings are literally hundreds of research findings that have a direct impact on our understanding of how children's brains develop.

This book takes some of those findings, explains how they affect children, and then offers suggestions for applying that information. A bibliography of children's books and suggestions for more in-depth reading are provided for each topic.

There are approximately 78,000 babies born in this country each week. That means we have 78,000 new opportunities weekly to help children strengthen and grow brain connections. What are we waiting for? Our generation is the first to be armed with the scientific knowledge of "how." Let's not miss our window of opportunity.

Parts of this introduction were taken from articles written by the author that appeared in Child Care Information Exchange, P. O. Box 2890, Redmond, WA 98073, 1-800-221-2864.

Sniff, Sniff
Aromas and the Brain

Our sense of smell is the only sense that sends information directly to the brain. Of the twelve nerve endings that enter the brain, only the olfactory (sense of smell) passes stimuli to the brain unfiltered. Researchers found that certain odors increase the ability to learn, create, and think. Other aromas are thought to boost attention and learning. Peppermint, basil, lemon, cinnamon, and rosemary are linked to mental alertness. Lavender, chamomile, orange, and rose promote relaxation and calming.

The chart on the next page shows some common conditions and the aromas that may help improve them.

CONDITION	EFFECTIVE HERB*
LOW ENERGY	Basil, cinnamon, clove, garlic, geranium, hyssop, marjoram, nutmeg, pine
ANXIETY	Basil, chamomile, eucalyptus, jasmine, marjoram, neroli, rose, thyme, ylang-ylang
DEPRESSION	Borneo camphor, chamomile, jasmine, lavender, nutmeg, thyme, verbena
IRRITABILITY	Chamomile, cypress, jasmine, lavender, marjoram, melissa, nutmeg, rose, vanilla, verbena
NERVES (GENERAL TONIC)	Chamomile, cinnamon, cypress, frankincense, jasmine, lavender, marjoram, neroli, nutmeg, orange, rose, sage, sandalwood, verbena
STRESS/FATIGUE	Basil, chamomile, cinnamon, clove, cypress, frankincense, jasmine, lavender, marjoram, neroli, orange, rose, sage, savory, sandalwood, thyme, vanilla

*Check for allergies to herbs and spices.

Ideas for Using Aromas to Build Brain Power

✸   Design cooking activities to release aromas that increase alertness. For example, cinnamon rolls, peppermint candies, and lemonade have aromas that encourage mental alertness.

Cinnamon Rolls
2 cups (480 ml) baking mix, such as Bisquick
⅔ cup (160 ml) milk
¼ cup (60 ml) sugar
margarine or butter
1 teaspoon ground cinnamon
cookie sheet, 2 small bowls, rolling pin, measuring cups, measuring spoons, table knife, breadboard

Combine baking mix and milk in a small bowl and beat with a fork. Place dough on a floured surface and knead gently. Roll into an 8" x 12" (20 cm x 30 cm) rectangle and spread with margarine. Mix sugar and cinnamon in another bowl and sprinkle over dough. Roll tightly and pinch ends closed. Cut into one-inch slices and place on greased cookie sheet. Bake 15 minutes at 425°F (220°C).

✳ Use scented playdough. Substituting one tablespoon of massage oil for one of the two tablespoons of oil suggested in most playdough recipes makes great scented playdough (see Scented Playdough Recipe #1). Flavored powdered drink mix, such as Kool-Aid, also creates a nicely scented playdough (see Scented Playdough Recipe #2).

Scented Playdough Recipe #1

3 cups (720 ml) flour
1½ (360 ml) cups salt
2 tablespoons oil (use 1 tablespoon of massage oil)
2 tablespoons cream of tartar
3 cups (720 ml) water
measuring cups and spoons, saucepan, mixing spoon, stove, or hot plate

Combine all ingredients in a saucepan. Cook over very low heat until mixture is no longer sticky to the touch. Add a teaspoon of flavored extract to make fragrant playdough.

Scented Playdough Recipe #2

1 package powdered drink mix, such as Kool-Aid
1 cup (240 ml) water
1 teaspoon baby oil
1 cup (240 ml) flour
½ cup (120 ml) salt
2 teaspoons cream of tartar
measuring cups and spoons, saucepan, mixing spoon, stove or hot plate, wax paper

Stir drink mix and water in a saucepan over medium heat until steam rises. Add baby oil and stir. Mix together remaining dry ingredients. Gradually add to heated liquids and stir until a mashed potato consistency is achieved. Remove from stove; place playdough on wax paper and knead until smooth. Allow to cool. Have fun!

✳ Encourage children to use scented markers for writing and drawing activities. Create your own colored markers by dipping dried-up markers in scented dyes or paints.

✳ Add cooking extracts to tempera paint, then ask children to make "scent-sational" paintings.

✳ Use potpourri. Children can make their own potpourri by placing cloves, cinnamon sticks, or scented cotton balls in a four-inch (ten-centimeter) square of netting, then tying it closed with a piece of ribbon.

✳ Provide hand lotions by the sink for children to use after washing their hands.

✳ Make scratch and sniff pictures. Mix gelatin using only half the amount of water called for in the recipe, then invite children to use it as paint. After the paint dries the children can scratch and sniff.

✳ Make perfume. Collect old flowers from a florist. Remove petals and place them in an empty orange juice can. Add enough water to cover petals. Put the orange juice can in a saucepan of water and warm on low heat for a couple of hours. Strain the liquid and bottle as perfume.

✳   Play florist. Put out flower pots, potting soil, and, if possible, discarded flowers from a florist for a realistic and aromatic touch.

✳   Grow an herb garden. Introduce children to various herbs and invite them to participate in cooking activities that will utilize the herbs.

✳   Fill beanbags with herbs.

✳   Take a nature walk. Encourage children to close their eyes and try to identify the smells of nature.

✳   Place calming or relaxing aromas in quiet areas and aromas that encourage alertness in more active areas.

✳   Make smelling bottles by dipping cotton balls in extracts and placing them in film canisters. Poke holes in the lids. Create two of each scent and encourage children to match the scents by using their sense of smell.

✳   Create scented crayons for children to use. Melt old and broken crayons in cans on a warming tray. Add extracts before the wax hardens.

✴ Make homemade toothpaste. Add water to baking soda until you have a paste consistency. Add a couple of drops of peppermint extract.

✴ Plant a rose garden or a flower bed and encourage children to help take care of it.

Books for children

Smelling Things by Allen Fowler
Nose Book by Al Perkins
Sniffing and Smelling by Henry Arthur Pluckrose
Smelling by Richard L. Allington

Want to read more?

Rechelbacher, Horst. 1987. *Rejuvenation: A Wellness Guide for Women and Men.* Rochester, VT: Thorsons Publishers.

Howard, Pierce J. 1994. *The Owner's Manual for The Brain: Everyday Applications from Mind-Brain Research.* Austin, TX: Leornian Press.

Eeeny, Meeney Miney, Mo

Choices and the Brain

When you offer children choices, especially about learning activities, they feel more posi- tive about their work and, at the same time, they feel less anxiety. High anxiety causes the release of hormones that inhibit learning while low anxiety enhances the learner's ability to learn. Positive feelings trigger the release of endorphins, which enhance the functioning of brain connections. Choices allow learners to reach self-determined goals, sparking and maintaining children's motivation, which is critical to learning.

Ideas for Using Choice to Build Brain Power

✻   Use sentence structures that suggest choices to children. For example, "You might try," or, "Perhaps another puzzle would be more challenging," instead of, "Do this."

✻   Keep the number of choices offered to three. Young children can become overwhelmed by too many choices.

✻   Offer children choices for snacks and meals.

✻   Help children recognize that there are inevitable consequences to the choices they make. Learning to accept responsibility for our choices is an important part of social-emotional development. Being allowed to experience the consequences of our choices is one of the quickest ways to learn to think through choices we make. For example, when children are offered a choice between several colors of paint and they choose the same color that one of their friends likes instead of choosing the best color to create their painting, they are left with the consequences of their choices. The important thing to remember is to let them experience the consequence; don't let them simply choose another color again. This kind of experience helps prepare children for later choices that will be harder and far more significant.

Another example: Ryan is asked to get ready for bed. He chooses to continue playing instead of doing as he was asked. The logical consequence of his choice is that tomorrow night he will have to prepare for bed earlier. The important thing to remember and to point out is that the choice not to follow instructions was his own. Getting ready for bed earlier is a consequence of his choice. It should not be viewed as punishment handed down by the adult. In the work world, when we make inappropriate choices, we are not allowed to point our finger at our boss. We are expected to assume responsibility for the choices we make.

✳ Use choices as often as possible when soliciting children's cooperation. For example, "Would you prefer chocolate milk or plain milk?"

✳ Encourage children to make their own choices when they spend allowance or gift money.

✳ Involve children in decision-making activities. Allow them a vote when choosing things like paint colors, snack and dinner menus, and where to hang a picture.

Ideas for Groups of Children

✳ Provide multiple activities so that children can have a choice of activities. For example, offer a variety of puzzles

instead of only one, or, if you want to develop hand-eye coordination, you might provide two options: Scissors with magazine pictures to cut out and tracing paper with patterns and markers for tracing.

✳   Invite children to help select sites for field trips, books to read, and activities for outdoors.

✳   Try money-making activities such as a sidewalk art sale or a carnival. Let children decide how to spend or donate the proceeds.

Books for children

More, More, More Said the Baby by Vera Williams
The Little Red Hen by Byron Barton
Peter's Chair by Ezra Jack Keats
David Decides about Thumb Sucking by Susan M. Heitler
"The Three Little Pigs" (any version)

Want to read more?

Deci, Edward, and Richard M. Ryan. 1985. *Intrinsic Motivation and Self Determination in Human Behavior*. New York: Plenum.

Glasser, William, and Karen Dotson. 1998. *Choice Theory in the Classroom*. New York: HarperCollins.

I Feel Blue

Color and the Brain

Brain researchers have verified that color affects our mood and behavior. Although this is not new information, the recent brain research has validated the earlier body of research.

Blues are calming and increase feelings of well-being, with sky-blue being the most tranquilizing color. When you see blue, your brain releases eleven neurotransmitters that bring relaxing calmness to the body. The effects can lower body temperature and reduce perspiration and appetite. Greens are also calming. Reds and yellows are energizing (these colors also encourage creativity). Red is an engaging and emotive color, so that an anxious person may be disturbed by red, while a calm person may be excited. Red triggers the

pituitary and adrenal glands, enhances the sense of smell, and can increase breathing and appetite. Yellow is the first color a person distinguishes in the brain. Brown promotes a sense of security and relaxation and reduces fatigue. A textured gray is neutral. Off-white, yellow, and beige are optimal for positive feeling. Darker colors lower stress and increase feelings of peacefulness.

COLOR	MOOD/BEHAVIOR
RED	Energizes, encourages creativity, increases breathing and appetite, enhances the sense of smell
YELLOW	Energizes, creates positive feeling, encourages creativity
BLUE	Calms, promotes sense of well-being, reduces perspiration, reduces apetite
GREEN	Calms, lowers stress, creates feeling of peacefulness
OFF-WHITE	Promotes positive feelings, optimal for learning
BROWN	Promotes relaxation and a sense of security, reduces fatigue
BEIGE	Promotes positive feelings

Ideas for Using Color to Build Brain Power

✳   Place calming colors (blues, beige tones, greens) in quiet or reflection areas. Stay away from bright colors.

✳   Choose colors for easel painting depending on children's moods.

✳   Invite children to use colored markers and colored pencils in their drawing and writing.

✳   Discuss the moods of colors with children. Do they agree with what people say about colors? Does blue make them feel calm? Does red excite them?

✳   Try your own color experiments. Do you notice mood or behavioral differences related to color? For example, try using reds to encourage appetite, blues to subdue appetite. Does it work?

✳   Discuss color-related phrases with children such as blue Monday, feeling blue, seeing red, and so on. Do the phrases and their meanings match the research findings?

Ideas for Groups of Children

✳ Challenge children to brainstorm solutions to a problem. Use a red marker to list the ideas.

✳ Let children dictate a story or recall the sequence of events during a field trip. Use colored chalk or markers to record their dictation.

✳ Use reds and yellows in the dramatic play, block, and art centers. Remember, these colors increase creativity.

✳ Hang crepe paper streamers from the ceiling where you wish to elicit specific moods (for example, dark colors in a reading area and bright colors in an art area).

✳ Discuss colors. Find out what everyone's favorite color is. See if children associate feelings with different colors.

✳ Think about the effect of color when planning activities such as children's parties. Too many bright colors may over-stimulate an already excited group of children.

✳ Invite children to create colored glasses. Cut a frame from tagboard or poster board and glue in colored cellophane lenses.

✴ Provide children with strips of colored cellophane. Encourage them to run outside in the sunshine holding the cellophane strips like a kite. Watch the colored "shadows" on the ground.

Books for children

Colors by Richard L. Allington
Is It Red? Is It Yellow? Is It Blue? by Tana Hoban
A Color of His Own by Leo Lionni
Red Is Best by Kathy Stinson

Want to read more?

Birren, Faber. 1997. *Color and Human Resources*. New York: Wiley.

Howard, Pierce J. 1994. *The Owner's Manual for The Brain: Everyday Applications from Mind-Brain Research*. Austin, TX: Leornian Press.

I Feel the Rhythm

Mind and Body Cycles and the Brain

Our minds and bodies have cycles that correspond to lunar (twenty-five hour) and solar (twenty-four hour) cycles. Blood pressure, mood swings, concentration, pulse rate, memory, and learning ability are all affected by lunar and solar cycles.

We breathe approximately fifteen times a minute.

Generally we breathe through one nostril for three hours, then after the tissue becomes engorged, we switch to the other nostril.

Our hearts beat once a second.

We blink five to fifteen times a minute.

Our brain's electrical rhythms occur one to twenty-five times a second.

Hormones are released into our bloodstream every two to four hours and dramatically affect our brain function. Researchers say that this release of hormones also affects our use of left and right hemispheres of the brain (see Cross-Lateral Movement, pages 55-62).

We have sleep and alert cycles that are with us around the clock. The middle of our sleep cycle will be mirrored twelve hours later by a period of drowsiness.

Between 9:00 a.m. and 11:00 a.m., the brain is fifteen percent more efficient for short-term memory. The process of integrating information into our long-term memory is generally more efficient in the afternoon.

The brain also has relaxation and energy cycles. Learning is best when cycled into "on" and "off" times. The "on" times should range from five to twenty minutes (depending upon the age of the learner) and the "off" times should be from two to five minutes. Below is a chart that lists common learning functions and mind and body cycle-related highs and lows:

LEARNING	CYCLE INFORMATION
SHORT-TERM MEMORY	Best in the morning
LONG-TERM MEMORY	Best in the afternoon
SLOW TIME	2:00 p.m. to 4:00 p.m.
INTELLECTUAL PERFORMANCE	Best in the late afternoon/early evening
COMPREHENSION	Increases as the day progresses
READING SPEED	Decreases as the day progresses

Ideas for Using Mind and Body Cycles to Build Brain Power

✳ Teach children to be aware of their biological rhythms. Put out a stethoscope and a stopwatch and encourage children to count their heartbeats per minute. Show them how to find their pulse. Encourage them to count breaths and blinks.

✳ Schedule active involvement activities between 2:00 p.m. and 4:00 p.m. to offset the biological slowdown time.

✳ Read books about lunar and solar cycles (seasons). Help children become aware of and see the influence of these cycles in nature. Call attention to seasonal changes. Observe the moon as it waxes and wanes.

✳ Be aware of your own biorhythms and watch for signs in children that will help you understand their cycles.

✳ Use the time from 5:00 p.m. to 7:00 p.m. to enhance relationships. This appears to be the appropriate time. It is interesting that it parallels our dinner time.

✳ Make sure children get adequate rest. Deep, profound rest helps with long-term memory.

✳ Teach things that require paying attention to detail in the mornings such as reading, listening, and observing. Allow afternoons to be more of a time for reflection and integration of concepts. Try projects, drama, and role play in the afternoon.

Ideas for Groups of Children

✳ Try scheduling assessment activities in the late afternoon when intellectual function is at its best.

✳ Remember that although we all have the same general cycles, the timing is slightly different for each individual. Researchers say we have a two- to four-hour variance.

Books for children

Sunshine Makes the Seasons by Franklyn M. Branley
Thirteen Moons on Turtle's Back by Joseph Bruchac
Everett Anderson's Year by Lucille Clifton
Ring of Earth by Jane Yolen
Goodnight Moon by Margaret Wise Brown
The Sun, The Moon, and The Stars by Mae Freeman

Want to read more?

Cambell, Don G., and Chris B. Brewer. 1991. *Rhythms of Learning: Creative Tools for Developing Lifelong Skills.* Tucson, AZ: Zephyr Press.
Orlock, Carol. 1993. *Inner Time.* New York: Birch Lane Press, Carol Publishing.

I Feel
I Remember

Emotions and the Brain

Emotions play an important role in both memory and motivation. Emotions are "housed" in the middle section of the brain. When incoming information is connected with an emotion, it receives a high priority for processing. It is, then, easy to see why we remember most easily the highs and lows of our lives. Researchers believe that this is because when emotions are present, hormones released by the brain act as a memory fixative. That's why emotions affect our retention. If you run through memories in your head you will notice that the memories more quickly accessed are the ones that are accompanied by emotions.

Several studies have demonstrated that motivation is also linked to emotions. Strong negative

emotions inhibit the learner's ability to think. For example, an argument at breakfast can distract the learner the rest of the day.

Top brain scientists say that emotions are a key part of the logic and reasoning processes. The brain makes better decisions when some emotion is present.

Ideas for Using Emotions to Build Brain Power

✳ Discuss the value of feelings. They help us work out sadness, share our joys, express our discontent, work out our problems and conflicts, calm our spirits, and balance our lives. Part of helping children attach emotion to learning is helping them understand and express emotions.

✳ Sing throughout the day. Songs generally fill us with positive emotion. Some songs are happy such as "Doodlely-Do," "If You're Happy and You Know It," and "The More We Get Together." Other songs are peaceful such as "Kum Ba Yah," "Twinkle, Twinkle Little Star," and "Tell Me Why." Still other songs are humorous, such as "The Little Skunk's Hole," "Boom, Boom, Ain't It Great to Be Crazy?" "Dirty Ole Bill," and "Hunk of Tin." A great book with a comprehensive collection of words to songs is *Rise Up Singing* edited by Peter Blood-Patterson. If you can't sing, then just hum a tune, or chant the words to songs.

"If You're Happy and You Know It"
(act out motions that words indicate)
If you're happy and you know it,
Clap your hands.
If you're happy and you know it,
Clap your hands.
If you're happy and you know it,

Then your face will surely show it.
If you're happy and you know it,
Clap your hands.

If you're happy and you know it,
Stomp your feet!
Pat your head!
Say hello!
(create as many verses as you like)

"The More We Get Together"

The more we get together, together,
    together.
The more we get together, the
    happier we'll be!
For your friends are my friends and
    my friends are your friends.
The more we get together, the
    happier we'll be!

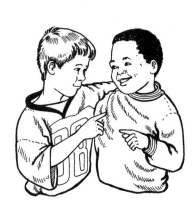

"Kum Ba Yah"

Kum ba ya, my Lord, Kum ba yah! (3 times)
Oh, Lord, Kum ba yah!

Someone's singing, Lord, Kum ba yah! (3 times)
Oh, Lord, Kum ba yah!

Someone's praying…, Someone's dreaming…
Someone's laughing…, Someone's crying…

"Twinkle, Twinkle Little Star"

Twinkle, twinkle, little star,
How I wonder what you are!
Up above the world so high,
Like a diamond in the sky.
Twinkle, twinkle, little star,
How I wonder what you are.

"Boom, Boom, Ain't It Great to Be Crazy?"
A horse and a flea and three blind mice,
Sat on a curbstone shooting dice,
The horse he slipped and fell on the flea,
"Whoops," said the flea, "There's a horse on me!"

Chorus:
Boom, boom, ain't it great to be crazy?
Boom, boom, ain't it great to be crazy?
Giddy and foolish the whole day through,
Boom, boom, ain't it great to be crazy?

Way down South where bananas grow,
A flea stepped on an elephant's toe.
The elephant cried with tears in his eyes,
"Why don't you pick on someone your
   size?"
(Chorus)

Way up North where there's ice and snow,
There lived a penguin and his name was
   Joe.
He got so tired of black and white,
He wore pink slacks to the dance last night.
(Chorus)

"Little Hunk of Tin"
I'm a little hunk of tin.
Nobody knows what shape
   I'm in.
Got four wheels and a running
   board.
I'm a four-door.
I'm a Ford.

Chorus (sing twice)
Honk, honk *(pull ear)*
Rattle, rattle. *(shake head)*
Crash, crash. *(push chin)*
Beep, beep. *(push nose)*

✴ Help children see the need for what they are learning. For example, the ability to read allows you to enjoy a story-book, follow rules for a game, know what your friend is saying in a letter, and determine which candy bar has your favorite ingredients. Math helps you know how many more days until your birthday, how much money you need to buy a new ball, and so on.

✴ Add surprises. Invite a funny or interesting character to "pop in" to deliver some important information.

✴ Use stories with emotional messages to help children learn concepts.

STORY	CONCEPT
ITSY BITSY SPIDER	Try, try again
THE TENTH GOOD THING ABOUT BARNEY	Death
AMAZING GRACE	Believing in yourself
A CHAIR FOR MY MOTHER	Cooperation, Respect, Love
ALEXANDER AND THE TERRIBLE, HORRIBLE, NO GOOD, VERY BAD DAY	Everyone has a bad day
OWL MOON	Father/child relationship, Nature
LOVE YOU FOREVER	Security
OWL BABIES	Fear
FEELINGS	Feelings
FROG IS FRIGHTENED	Fear
MAMA ZOOMS	Fun with Mom
GOING HOME	Celebration

✳   Teach stress-relaxation strategies such as deep breathing, thinking of a peaceful place, and exercising. Relieving stress helps us tap into positive emotions.

✳   Let children know you care about them.

✳   Express your emotions openly. Let children see you happy, sad, angry, peaceful, and content.

✳   Discuss the emotional events of your life such as your high school graduation, a recent wedding, or a family picnic. If there are photographs, show them to the children.

✳   When talking about memories of events, ask children if they can remember how they felt at the time. Ask them how the memory makes them feel now.

✳   Discuss the emotions involved in celebrations. Count and describe the many emotions in celebrating a new birth, wedding, birthday, or holiday.

Ideas for Groups of Children

✳   Use drama. Children love puppets, role play, and acting. Their emotional interaction will help them remember and learn the message of the story.

Books for children

A Chair for My Mother by Vera B. Williams
Alexander and the Terrible, Horrible, No Good, Very Bad Day by
    Judith Viorst
Owl Moon by Jane Yolen
Owl Babies by Martin Waddell
Feelings by Joanne Murphy
Love You Forever by Robert Munsch
Amazing Grace by Mary Hoffman
Frog Is Frightened by Max Velthuijs
Mama Zooms by Jane Cowen-Fletcher
Going Home by Eve Bunting
The Kissing Hand by Audrey Penn

Want to read more?

Davis, Joel. 1997. *Mapping the Mind: The Secrets of the Human Brain and How It Works*. Secaucus, NJ: Birch Lane Press.
Dumas, Lynne S. 1998. "IQ vs. EQ: Brains Aren't Everything." *Parents Magazine* 73:140.
Goleman, Daniel. 1995. *Emotional Intelligence*. New York: Bantam.
Ratnesar, Romesh. 1997. "Teaching Feelings." *Time* 150:62.

Hop, Skip Jump

Exercise and the Brain

We know that regular exercise is good for the body, and now we know that exercise is also good for the brain. There are many studies that document the overall benefits of exercise, but the benefits for the brain are clear and simple: exercise increases the flow of blood and oxygen to the brain. People who exercise regularly have improved short-term memory and exhibit faster reaction time. Exercisers also demonstrate higher levels of creativity than non-exercisers.

As an added bonus, physical exercise creates a quick rise and fall of adrenaline that parallels the rise and fall of adrenaline that occurs when we face challenges or problems. Adrenaline heightens our perceptions, speeds up heart rates, and prepares our bodies for fight or flight. The chemical reactions that occur during exercise provide practice for the similar responses needed in challenging situations.

Ideas for Using Exercise to Build Brain Power

✳   Use music and movement every day. Try exercise records and remember that dance is also a great form of exercise.

✳   Teach about health and fitness. Focus on the effects of exercise on both mental and physical abilities.

✳   Provide a stethoscope and invite children to listen to their hearts beat. Encourage children to do twenty-five jumping jacks and then use the stethoscope to listen to their heart beats a second time.

✳   Make exercise bands from three-foot lengths of one-inch (three-centimeter) wide elastic. Provide each child with an exercise band and try the following. Stand on part of the band and use your hands to stretch it over your head. Hold the band in front of you and stretch it across your chest. Place the band over your head and behind your neck. Stretch your hands forward. Create your own stretches.

✳ Play Left/Right Games. Toss a soft ball at a child and yell "left shoulder." The child tries to hit the ball with her left shoulder. Toss again and yell right foot, right elbow, left knee, and so on.

✳ Create an exercise program and schedule an exercise time daily or at least several times a week.

✳ Model exercising such as running laps on a playground or taking hikes or bike rides.

✳ Take children to a local gym, YMCA, or YWCA and demonstrate how the various exercise machines work.

✳ Encourage children to participate in dance classes or athletic activities such as playing soccer or swimming.

Books for children

From Head to Toe by Eric Carle
Shake It to the One That You Love the Best by Cheryl Warren
    Mattox
Clap Your Hands by Lorinda B. Cauley

Want to read more?

Brierley, John Keith. 1994. *Give Me a Child Until He Is Seven: Brain Studies and Early Childhood Education*. Bristol, PA: Falmer Press.

Water, Water Everywhere

Hydration and the Brain

The brain needs to be properly hydrated in order to be alert. Children who do not get enough water may appear bored, listless, and drowsy. Researchers recommend that we drink eight to fifteen glasses of water a day. Coffee, tea, and many sodas contain caffeine, which acts as a diuretic and reduces the hydration of the body and the brain. The body identifies fruit juices as a food because of their sugar content. The body triggers the digestive process, which also drains water from the body. None of these "water substitutes" provides proper hydration. Both deplete the body of fluids. Only water gets the job done. Drinking bottled water will insure that the water is free of contaminants.

Ideas for Building Brain Power With Hydration

✳   Model drinking water. Children learn more from our actions than from our words.

✳   Discuss drinking water with children. Explain in simple terms how water helps our brains work better. Our bodies, including our brains, need carbon, oxygen, nitrogen, and hydrogen to function effectively. Water is a combination of hydrogen and oxygen, two of these essential elements, and is used in the brain to make neurotransmitters (chemical impulses) which carry information between neurons.

✳   Take scheduled water breaks.

✳   Let children have water when they ask for it. At first they will need to go to the bathroom more frequently but eventually their bladders will adjust. Keep water available all day long. Serve water with meals and snacks.

✳   Provide small cups and encourage children to decorate their cups in their own unique fashion. Keep the cups accessible for drinking water.

✳   Provide straws and two cups of water. Encourage children to drink the water until one cup is half full and the other cup is empty. Do the same activity, changing the focus to counting sips of water. How many sips of water are in the cup? If children aren't counting yet have them use tally marks.

✳   Color ice cubes using food coloring or natural dyes such as juice from strawberries or blueberries.* Provide tongs and invite children to first sort the cubes by color, then eat the ice cubes.

✳   Provide ice cubes in a zip-closure bag and give children a block to make crushed ice. Invite children to eat the results of their crushing. This is also a good way to learn about force.

✳   Provide ice in a zip-closure bag and encourage children to see if holding the ice on different items, like a book, a mitten, a crayon, or a mirror will make the item cold. Do some items get colder than others? When the children are finished with the experiment and the ice is melted, let them pour the water through a funnel into a cup and drink it.

✳   Invite children to place ice cubes in two zip-closure bags. Have them place one bag in a sunny window and the other in a cool place. Which one melts first? After the ice melts let the children drink the water.

* Researchers believe that dyes, especially the combination of several dyes, may negatively impact learning and behavior in a small percentage of people. Dyes appear to have no effect on the majority of people, but on others they can create problems both with concentration and control.

✳ Let the children build and sculpt with shaved ice and then encourage them to eat their creation. (Wash hands first.)

✳ Encourage children to drink water when they brush their teeth. This creates an opportunity to add drinking water to an existing routine.

✳ Demonstrate the effect of water on plants. Provide two plants. Water one on a regular basis and don't water the second one at all. After a week or so, maybe sooner, the effect on the plant that didn't receive water should be visible.

Ideas for Groups of Children

✳ Invite children to have a contest with a friend to see who can hold a mouthful of water for the longest amount of time.

✳ Encourage children to drink water from a long straw and a short straw. Have a contest. Let one child drink eight ounces (240 ml) of water with a long straw and another child with a short straw. What happens? (Make a very long straw by taping several straws together.)

✳   Provide crazy straws and see who can empty a glass of water first using their crazy straw.

Books for children

Water by J.M. Parramon
The Water's Journey by Eleanor Schmid
Water is Wet by Penny Pollock

Want to read more?

Dennison, Paul, and Gail Dennison. 1988. *Brain Gym.* Teacher's Ed. Ventura, CA: Edu-kinesthetics.
Ward, C., and Jan Jaley. 1993. *Learning to Learn.* New Zealand: A&H Print Consultants.

Laughter and Learning

Laughter and the Brain

Laughter increases white blood cell activity and changes the chemical balance of the blood. This is believed to boost the body's production of chemicals needed for alertness and memory. Laughter reduces stress, and low stress enhances the brain's receptivity to learning. According to researchers, laughing (having fun) also boosts the body's immune system for three days—the day of the fun and the next two.

Ideas for Using Laughter to Build Brain Power

✳ Sing silly songs (see pages 35-37, 56-57). Here are some songs children find humorous:

"Down by the Bay"
Down by the bay
Where the watermelons grow.
Back to my home
I dare not go.
For if I do
My mother will say,
"Did you ever see a bear coming
    his hair?"
Down by the bay.

Sing the song again using a bee with a sunburned knee, moose kissing a goose, whale with a polka dot tail, and so on. Let the children make up verses.

"Catalina Magnalina"
She had a peculiar name but she wasn't to blame.
She got it from her mother, whose the same, same, same.
(Chorus)
Catalina Magnalina, Hootensteiner Bogentwiner
Hogan Logan Bogan was her name.

She had two peculiar teeth in her mouth,
One pointed north and the other pointed south.
(Chorus)

She had two peculiar eyes in her head,
One was purple and the other was red.
(Chorus)

Add your own verses.

"Oh, I Wish I Were"

Oh, I wish I were a little juicy orange, (echo, juicy orange)
Oh, I wish I were a little juicy orange, (juicy orange)
I'd go sqirty, squirty, squirty,
Over everybody's shirty,
Oh I wish I were a little juicy orange.
  (juicy orange)

Oh, I wish I were a little bar of soap, (bar
  of soap)
Oh, I wish I were a little bar of soap, (bar
  of soap)
I'd go slidy, slidy, slidy,
Over everybody's body,
Oh, I wish I were a little bar of soap. (bar
  of soap)

Oh, I wish I were a little glob of mud,
  (glob of mud)
Oh, I wish I were a little glob of mud,
  (glob of mud)
I'd go oozy, oozy, oozy,
Over everybody's shoezzy.
Oh, I wish I were a little glob of mud.
  (glob of mud)

Oh, I wish I were a little cookie crumb,
  (cookie crumb)
Oh, I wish I were a little cookie crumb,
  (cookie crumb)
I'd go crummy, crummy, crummy,
Over everybody's tummy.
Oh, I wish I were a little cookie crumb.
  (cookie crumb)

Oh I wish I were a little radio, (radio)
Oh, I wish I were a little radio, (radio)
I'd go click!

CLICK

✳   Read humorous books such as *Once Upon MacDonald's Farm* by Stephen Gammel, *Caps for Sale* by Esphyr Solbodkina, *Moira's Birthday* by Robert Munsch, *Thomas' Snowsuit* by Robert Munsch, and *Wacky Wednesday* by Theodore LeSieg.

✳   Support and encourage children's natural clowning around. Sometimes we are quick to stop behavior that really isn't causing any harm. A quick laugh will reduce stress and boost learning.

✳   Laugh at children's attempts to be funny.

✳   Laugh at yourself when you do something silly. Laugh with children when they do something silly.

✳   Put funny pictures on the refrigerator.

✳   Share simple jokes. There are some very simple joke books available for children. Check one out. Make up simple jokes, riddles, or limericks with children.

✳   Use humor. Wear roller skates one day. Invite children to work puzzles under the table. Create a tunnel out of boxes and place it at the front door so that children will have to crawl into and out of the tunnel. Invite a clown to spend time with you.

✳   Play "What If." What if pigs could fly? What if your family pet was an elephant? What if children were in charge of parents?

✳ Share appropriate cartoons with children. Read the funny papers with children.

✳ Share stories about funny things.

✳ Keep the atmosphere light. Avoid things that are depressing such as the evening news, focusing on stories of other peoples' problems, or heavy TV drama. A little of the heavy stuff goes a long way.

✳ Hang around people who are "up" (happy).

Ideas for Groups of Children

✳ Try tummy ticklers. Children lie on the floor, each placing his head on another child's tummy. Invite the children to start laughing. It's contagious. Soon everyone will be giggling.

✳ Play "You Can't Make Me Laugh." Children sit in a circle. IT stands in the center of the circle and tries to make the other children laugh. The child who laughs first becomes the new IT.

Books for children

Once Upon Macdonald's Farm by Stephen Gammell
Moira's Birthday by Robert Munsch
Thomas' Snowsuit by Robert Munsch
The King Who Reigned by Fred Gwynne
Caps for Sale by Esphyr Slobodkina
Wacky Wednesday by Theodore LeSieg
Alexander and the Terrible, Horrible, No Good, Very Bad Day by
    Judith Viorst
Imogene's Antlers by David Small
Falling Up by Shel Silverstein
Muddle Cuddle by Laurel Dee Gugler
Silly Sally by Audrey Wood

Want to read more?

Cousins, Norman. 1989. *Head First: The Biology of Hope*. New York: Dutton.

Fry, William F. Jr., and Walleed A. Salanch. 1993. *Advances in Humor and Psychotherapy*. Sarasota, FL: Professional Resource Exchange, Inc.

Always Across

Cross-Lateral Movement and the Brain

Doing arm and leg movements that cross over from one side of the body to the other (cross-lateral movements) can have a dramatic effect on learning. Since the left side of the brain controls the right side of the body and the right side of the brain controls the left side of the body, the two sides of the brain are forced to communicate when the legs and arms cross over.

Our learning and performance are dramatically affected by our biological rhythm. We have cycles of the mind and body that correspond to lunar and solar cycles (see page 30). Brain research tells us that every ninety minutes the normal hormone levels of our bodies peak. This peak causes the brain to get stuck on the right side or the left side. The use of cross-lateral movement is an easy way to "unstick" the brain. We need to engage both sides of the brain to learn efficiently and effectively.

Ideas for Using Cross-Lateral Movements to Build Brain Power

✳ Start each day with exercises that require cross-lateral movements, such as twisting at the waist with arms stretched to the side and bending at the waist to touch toes using left hand to touch right toe and right hand to touch left toe.

✳ Sing songs and repeat chants using hand motions that cross the midline of the body such as "Doodlely-Do," "Hot Cross Buns," and "Pat-a-Cake."

"Doodlely-Do"

Perform these movements in rhythm with this chant. Clap thighs twice. Clap hands twice. Cross hands in front of you four times (left hand on top twice, then right hand on top twice). Touch nose, then right shoulder with left hand. Touch nose, then left shoulder with right hand. Move hands in "talking" motion just above shoulders, then above head. Repeat throughout the song.

Please sing to me that sweet
   melody
Called Doodlely-Do, Doodlely-Do.
I like the rest, but the one I like
   best
Goes Doodlely-Do, Doodlely-Do.
It's the simplest thing, there isn't
   much to it.
All you gotta do is Doodlely-Do it.
I like it so that wherever I go
It's the Doodlely, Doodlely-Do.

"Hot Cross Buns"

Partners stand facing each other. Slap knees, clap hands, touch right hands, slap knees, clap hands, touch left hands. Repeat once, then end with slap knees, clap hands, and touch both hands together.

Hot cross buns.
Hot cross buns.
One a penny,
Two a penny,
Hot cross buns.

✳   Vary movements to traditional songs such as "Itsy Bitsy Spider" and "Where Is Thumbkin?"

"Where Is Thumbkin?"

When you bring hands out from behind back, bring them across your midline. It will result in hands being crossed in front of your chest as the fingers talk to each other.

Where is Thumbkin? *(hands behind back)*
Where is Thumbkin?
Here I am. Here I am. *(bring out right thumb, then left)*
How are you today, sir? *(bend right thumb)*
Very well, I thank you. *(bend left thumb)*
Run away. *(put right thumb behind back)*
Run away. *(put left thumb behind back)*

"Itsy Bitsy Spider"

The itsy, bitsy spider went up the water spout.
  (use right hand to crawl up left arm)
Down came the rain and washed the spider out. *(swoosh hands down diagonally from left to right and then from right to left)*
Out came the sun and dried up all the rain. *(make a big circle using both arms)*
And the itsy, bitsy spider climbed up the spout again. *(use right hand to crawl up left arm)*

✳ Make up hand jives. For example, slap right hand on left knee and then clap hands in the center of the body. Slap left hand on right knee and clap hands. Then snap fingers several times while crossing hand over hand, left over right and then right over left. Repeat sequence.

✳ Play records that focus on body movements. If crossing the midline is not inherent in the prescribed motions, add motions that include cross-lateral movements.

✳ Teach children simple dances from the fifties and sixties like the Twist, the Pony, and the Stroll. Each dance includes steps that require crossing the midline.

✳ Dance using streamers and scarves. Encourage children to swing them across their bodies.

✳ Play waltz music. Invite children to remove their shoes and socks and skate. Encourage them to swing their arms in front of them.

✳ Walk on a balance beam. If you don't have a balance beam, use a strip of masking tape on the floor.

✳ Go to the park. Play on the jungle gym. Challenge the children to use cross-lateral movements as they climb the ladder to the sliding board, reaching their left arm across to the right side of the ladder and vice versa as they climb.

✳ Encourage children to climb trees.

✳ Take a brisk walk outside. Encourage children to swing their arms as they walk.

✳ Encourage children to stop occasionally and give themselves a couple of hugs (cross arms across the chest and squeeze) or pats on the back (left hand to right shoulder and right hand to left shoulder).

✳ Rearrange materials on tables so children must reach across the mid-line to grasp what they need.

✳ Encourage children to paint with both hands at the easel.

✳ Play games that require children to crawl on the floor and challenge them to crawl in such a way as to use cross-lateral movement.

✳ Teach children to tell and act out stories that require cross-lateral hand movements. For example, here's a cute one:

Mr. Wiggle and Mr. Waggle

This is Mr. Wiggle (*hold up right fist with the thumb pointing up—wiggle thumb*), and this is Mr. Waggle (*hold up left fist with thumb pointing up—wiggle thumb*). Mr. Wiggle and Mr. Waggle live in houses on top of different hills and three hills apart. (*Put thumbs inside of fists.*)

One day, Mr. Wiggle decided to visit Mr. Waggle. He opened his door (*open fist*), pop, came outside (*raise thumb*), pop, and closed his door (*close fist*), pop. Then he went down the hill and up the hill, down the hill and up the hill, and down the hill and up the hill (*move right thumb down and up in a wave fashion to go with text*).

When he reached Mr. Waggle's house he knocked on the door, knock, knock, knock (*use right thumb to tap left fist*). No one answered. So, Mr. Wiggle went down the hill and up the hill, and down the hill and up the hill, and down the hill and up the hill to his house (*use wave motion to follow text*). When he reached his house he opened the door (*open fist*), pop, went inside (*place thumb in palm*), pop, and closed the door (*close fist*), pop.

The next day Mr. Waggle decided to visit Mr. Wiggle. He opened his door *(open left fist)*, pop, came outside *(raise thumb)*, pop, and closed his door *(close fist)*, pop. Then he went down the hill and up the hill, down the hill and up the hill and down the hill and up the hill *(move thumb down and up in a wave fashion to go with text)*.

When he reached Mr. Wiggle's house, he knocked on the door, knock, knock, knock *(use left thumb to tap right fist)*. No one answered. So, Mr. Waggle went down the hill and up the hill, and down the hill and up the hill, and down the hill and up the hill to his house *(use wave motion to follow text)*. When he reached his house, he opened the door *(open fist)*, pop, went inside *(place thumb in palm)*, pop, and closed the door *(close fist)*, pop.

The next day Mr. Wiggle *(shake right fist)* decided to visit Mr. Waggle and Mr. Waggle *(shake left fist)* decided to visit Mr. Wiggle at the same time. So, they opened their doors *(open both fists)*, pop, went outside *(raise thumbs)*, and closed their doors *(close fists)*, pop, and went down the hill and up the hill, and down the hill and up the hill *(wave motion to follow text)*, and they met on top of the hill.

They talked and laughed (wiggle thumbs) and visited until the sun went down. Then they went down the hill and up the hill, and down the hill and up the hill, to their own homes *(wave motion with both hands to text)*. They opened their doors *(open fists)*, pop, went inside *(tuck thumbs inside)*, pop, and closed the doors *(close fists)*, pop, and went to sleep. *(Place your head on your hands.)*

✳ Invite children to help with simple housekeeping chores. Jobs like washing windows and cleaning mirrors require cross-lateral movement.

✳ Encourage children to sit on your lap and read the funny paper with you. Let children turn the pages of the paper, a cross-lateral movement.

✳ Encourage children to use a punching bag. You can create your own bag by stuffing a pillowcase with old nylons or rags, tying it shut, and hanging it from the ceiling. (Great for reducing stress and channeling anger, too.)

Ideas for Groups of Children

✳ Make friendship circles. Provide a large sheet of butcher paper and crayons and invite children to make large interlocking circles with a friend.

✳ Play outdoor games that encourage cross-lateral movement such as jump rope and swinging statues. One child is the *swinger*. The *swinger* uses both hands to hold one hand of another child and then swings the child around two or three times before letting go. The object of the game is for the child who was swung to freeze like a statue in the position he lands in until the swinger counts to ten. If the child who is the statue moves before the number ten is reached, she becomes the new *swinger*. Be sure to play this game in an open area. Play Down in the Valley, a jump rope game. Two children hold opposite ends of a rope and gently swing it back and forth. The rest of the children form a line and individually attempt to jump over the rope as it is swung. Children who miss become swingers.

✳ Teach simple square dance steps. The do-si-do and promenade provide great cross-lateral movements. Make up new dances using square dance steps.

✳ Encourage children to create puppet shows. Moving puppets across the stage will require crossing the midline.

✳ Teach children how to shake hands and to double shake (left hand to friend's left hand and right hand to friend's right hand). Stop several times a day to shake hands with a friend.

✳ Invite children to form a friendship circle. Have them stand in a circle, cross their arms right over left, and hold the hands of the children standing on each side of them. Encourage children to say something nice about a friend. When finished have them turn under their right arm and let go of each others' hands as they complete the turn.

Books for children

Hand Rhymes by Marc Brown
Dance, Tanya by Patricia Lee Gauch
Clap Your Hands by Lorinda Bryan Cauley
Skates by Ezra Jack Keats
Every Time I Climb a Tree by David McCord
Song and Dance Man by Karen Ackerman

Want to read more?

Dennison, Paul, and Gail Dennison. 1988. *Brain Gym*. Teacher's Ed. Ventura, CA: Edu-kinesthetics.
Springer, Sally and Greg Deutsch. 1998. *Left Brain Right Brain*. New York: W.H. Freeman and Company.

Many Ways to be Smart

Multiple Intelligences and the Brain

Thanks to the work of Howard Gardner (Frames of Mind: The Theory of Multiple Intelligences, 1983), we have come to accept the idea that there are multiple ways to demonstrate intelligence or high ability. Prior to Gardner's work it was assumed that intelligence was measured only in terms of linguistic and mathematical abilities. Dr. Gardner claims there are many ways of expressing intelligence. He has identified and validated eight intelligences: Linguistic (word smart), Logical Mathematical (logic smart), Spatial (picture smart), Bodily Kinesthetic (body smart), Musical (music smart), Interpersonal (people smart), Intrapersonal (self smart), and Naturalist (nature smart).

It is generally accepted that intelligence is the ability to see patterns and draw relationships from past patterns to

future learning. Looking at intelligence from Gardner's perspective, individuals who are linguistically smart see the patterns in language in such a way that they are highly competent at putting words together in written and oral fashion. Likewise, individuals who are interpersonally smart see the patterns in human behavior and are highly competent in understanding how to work with people based on their observations of patterns of behavior. Because individuals are unique in expressing their intellect and all types of intellect are necessary for a functional society, we need to focus activities in all the areas of intelligences.

Current research verifies that the eight multiple intelligences are highly interrelated but at the same time autonomous in the brain areas dedicated to processing individual intelligences' function. For example, linguistic intelligence is processed in the left temporal and frontal lobe of the brain. For most people musical intelligence is processed in the right hemisphere. Spatial intelligence is processed in the posterior regions of the right hemisphere and so forth. New technology has assisted in fine tuning the exact location of processing. In addition, the recent brain research suggests that a person's innate brain capabilities and childhood experiences combine to develop each form of intelligence to its basic functional level of problem-solving.

Ideas for Using Multiple Intelligences to Build Brain Power

 Invite children to tell or write stories from their points of view.

✳ Ask questions that allow children to reflect on their own experiences and tie those experiences to new information. For example, after listening to the story of "Little Red Riding Hood," you might ask the children if they recall a time when they broke a rule. What happened? What did it feel like? Or, when talking about colors, you might ask what moods different colors create for them.

✳ Encourage children to look for patterns in language, math, movement, art, behavior, and feelings (see Patterns and the Brain, pages 85-93).

✳ Invite children to use sculpture, shadow boxes, and models to show what they know or what they like.

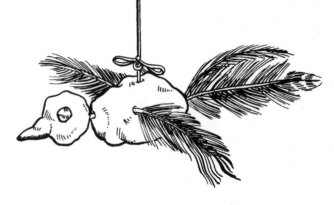

✳ Allow children to record their own stories and messages on a tape recorder. It's great for language development and organizing speech.

✳ Encourage journal writing.

✳ Use colorful markers and ink pens for drawing and writing.

✳ Try using guided imagery with children. They love to travel in their imagination.

✳ Use songs, finger plays, raps, and chants.

✳ Provide choices as often as possible. It empowers all children and is particularly appealing to the intrapersonal child.

✳ Use mood music as a background at quiet times throughout the day.

✳   Encourage children to become involved in sports activities, music lessons, art lessons, drama groups, and so on. All of these activities enhance the development of children's ability.

✳   Work puzzles with children.

✳   Invite children to help cook a snack or meal. Let them be involved in the entire process: selecting what will be fixed (considering likes and dislikes), shopping for ingredients (organizing resources), preparing the food (math skills), and serving the meal (artistic presentation).

✳   Challenge children to find patterns in routines, behaviors, activities, seasons, stories, and so forth (see Patterns and the Brain, pages 85-93).

✳   Encourage children to solve their own problems. Problem solving allows children to practice a variety of skills within a meaningful context and often provides opportunities for working on negotiating and compromising (see Problem Solving, pages 97-104).

✳   Invite children to help read the map on road trips. Help them create maps of their rooms—then maps illustrating the path from home to school.

✳   Teach children to value their unique intelligences and to recognize the value of all the intelligences. It takes all abilities to keep our society prosperous.

✳   Encourage children to join groups that promote camaraderie and the building of relationships such as Blue Birds and YMCA/YWCA programs.

✳   Read a variety of materials to children—newspaper articles, poems, books, and magazine articles, if appropriate. Be sure to end the day with a bedtime story.

Ideas for Groups of Children

✳   Provide opportunities for children to use role play and puppet dramatization to express ideas, feelings, and concepts, or review conceptual material.

✳   Help children rewrite stories as plays. Encourage them to act out their new version.

✳   Play games like Simon Says, Charades, and Outburst.

✳   Practice skills of negotiation. Teach children how to resolve conflict by negotiation and compromise.

✳   Play cooperative games such as Cooperative Musical Chairs, Tug of Peace, and Pretzel Pass. These games build interpersonal relationships.

Cooperative Musical Chairs
Place chairs as you normally would for musical chairs (one chair per child). Remove one or two chairs after the first round. When the music stops the second time, even though there are not enough chairs, the children will need to figure out how everyone can have a seat. (Examples include pushing chairs together to make a bigger chair, sitting in the lap of another child, and

sharing chairs.) Remove additional chair(s) each time the music stops. The game continues as long as there is space for everyone to sit down when the music stops.

Tug of Peace

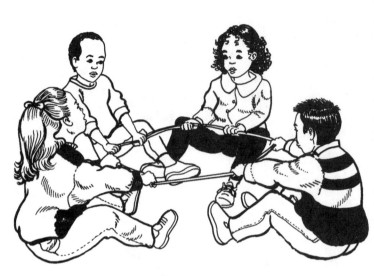

Tie the ends of a long piece of rope (approximately twelve to eighteen inches or thirty to forty-five centimeters per child) to make a circle. Ask the children to sit on the floor around the outside of the rope. Suggest that each child grab the rope and use it to pull up to a standing position. (Practice in a small group, then move to the entire group.)

Pretzel Pass

Instruct children to sit or stand in a circle. Provide each child with a straw, chopstick, or dowel rod. Put a large pretzel on every other stick. Invite the children to pass the pretzels around the circle using only their stick until everyone has a pretzel or until the music stops. (Any circular snack may be used for this activity.)

✳   Graph choices (who likes peanut butter and jelly sandwiches) or situations (how many children are wearing red and how many are wearing green) whenever possible. It's a great visual organization.

✳   Use manipulatives to learn one-to-one correspondence, graph results of an activity, or just for playing.

✳   Obtain a book of brain teasers. Select one brain teaser for each week. Let the solver select the next challenge.

✳   Provide opportunities for brainstorming. For example, how else could this story have ended? What other ways can you use a clothespin? Where can we go on our field trip?

Books for children

Leo the Late Bloomer by Robert Kraus
I Like Me by Nancy Carlson
Josefina by Jeanette Winter
Song and Dance Man by Karen Ackerman
The Little Painter of Sabana Grande by Patricia M. Markun
I Can Hear the Sun by Patricia Polacco

Want to read more?

Armstrong, Thomas. 1993. *Seven Kinds of Smart: Identifying and Developing Your Many Intelligences.* Alexandria, VA: Association for Supervision and Curriculum Development.

Armstrong, Thomas. 1994. *Multiple Intelligences in the Classroom.* Alexandria, VA: Association for Supervision and Curriculum Development.

Gardner, Howard. 1983. *Frames of Mind: The Theory of Multiple Intelligences.* New York: Basic Books.

Nicholson, Kristen. 1998. *Developing Students' Multiple Intelligences.* New York: Scholastic.

Phipps, Patricia A. 1997. *Multiple Intelligences in the Early Childhood Classroom.* Worthington, OH: SRA/McGraw-Hill.

Start With Mozart

Music and the Brain

All early sounds, including music and rhythms, play a profound role in shaping the brain. The positive effect music has on brain development is a very popular area of brain research. Although people seem happy to hop on the music bandwagon, we must interpret the research accurately and take care not to oversimplify or overgeneralize. There are a number of studies related to music and brain research. There is evidence that listening to music (and, for older children, learning a musical instrument) can boost memory, attention, motivation, and learning. It can also lower stress, activate both sides of the brain, and increase spatial temporal reasoning.

Some of the most well-known studies include the following:

✳ Jean Houston, leading pioneer of the effect of

music on physical and mental abilities, states that music "raises the molecular structure of the body." Music does this because it has its own wave length frequency. When music resonates with our body rhythms it has a powerful influence on our alertness and our ability to learn. Most classical music is in tune with our body rhythms.

✸ Webb and Webb say that "music rhythms, patterns, contrasts, and varying tonalities encode any new information." The researchers believe that music is a powerful way to present information.

✸ Scartelli reports that music is a mood enhancer. Favorite songs boost endorphins; endorphins boost attention and memory.

✸ Clynes says that there is greater consistency in the body's pulse response to classical music than to rock.

✸ A research study by Graziano et al. (1997) validates the effect of piano lessons on spatial temporal reasoning. Four-year-old children who took six months of piano keyboard lessons scored thirty percent higher on temporal spatial activities than their peers who received six months of singing or computer lessons.

The term "Mozart effect" comes from several studies regarding the effect that listening to Mozart has on brain activity. Participants demonstrated increased abilities in spatial learning, memory, and reasoning. In studies that included preschoolers and junior- and senior-level college students, researchers found that the brain activity had striking similarities to the written score of Mozart-composed music. Since the patterns in Mozart's music are parallel to the patterns the brain uses as it connects synapses, is it possible that our brains are biologically receptive to certain music?

Studies suggest that listening to music during the first three years of life helps the brain form patterns that are essential to the learning process. The brain adapts easily during the early years, so a wide variety of music should *be introduced. There is no concert-level performer in recorded history who began training after the age of ten.*

Ideas for Using Music to Build Brain Power

✳   Sing a song, any song, every morning to start the day.

✳   Use songs to introduce information. For example, use "Itsy Bitsy Spider" (page 57) to learn about spiders, "Twinkle, Twinkle Little Star" (page 36) to learn about nighttime, and "Rain, Rain, Go Away" to learn about weather.

✳   Play marching music and invite children to create different marching steps such as high steps, fast steps, long steps.

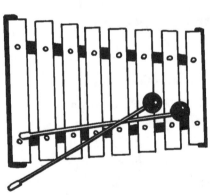

✳   Play a xylophone. Invite children to stand as the notes go up the scale and sit as the notes go down the scale.

✳   Invite children to move with streamers or scarves to the rhythm of music.

✳   Make homemade band instruments. For example, rubber bands and a shoe box make a great guitar, paper plates and kernels of popcorn make a good maraca, a spoon and a pie pan make a cymbal, and a stick and a box make a drum.

✳   Provide musical instruments for exploration. Xylophones, piano keyboards, autoharps, and drums are all intriguing to children and great for exploring notes, tones, and chords.

✳ Provide books based on songs, such as "The Wheels on the Bus" by Raffi and "Itsy Bitsy Spider" by Iza Trapani.

✳ Invite children to listen to a variety of music and then select music for the background of a story. For example, use scary music for when the wolf comes to the doors of the three pigs and happy music when the pigs are safe.

✳ Visit a high school band or orchestra. If possible, invite children to sit among the musicians. Does the music sound different when you are in the middle of the instruments?

✳ Do your own experiment. Try playing Mozart before working puzzles or before a thinking activity like brainstorming.

✳ Create a special music appreciation time a couple of times each week. Explore different types of music.

✳ Sing, sing, sing to unborn and newborn children.

✳ Play music tapes in the car. Use a variety of selections.

✳ Offer music lessons to children who are interested. The best time for music instruction is between the ages of three and ten.

✳ Take children to symphonies and operas that are appropriate. Many places offer special performances just for children.

✳ Model a love for music. Individuals who truly love music listen to it more and therefore enjoy the positive effects associated with music.

Ideas for Groups of Children

✳ Sing "The Alphabet Song" and "Twinkle, Twinkle, Little Star." Ask children how the songs are alike (they have the same tune) and how they are different (they have different words).

✳ Play Musical Ball Pass. Pass a ball while music is playing. When the music stops, the child holding the ball is caught. That child sits down. Continue passing the ball until only one child remains. (Try funny ways to pass the ball like between your legs, over your head, behind your back.)

✳ Play Musical Hide and Seek. Select a child to be IT. Ask IT to leave the room, then hide an object like a ball or a beanbag somewhere in the room. When IT returns start singing a song. Sing it loud when IT is near the object and softly when IT is not close. Continue until the object is found.

✳ Roll a ball to music. Have children sit in a circle and spread their legs until their toes are touching their neighbors on each side. Try rolling the ball to music with different tempos.

✳ Use songs for transitions. Some suggestions:

Clean-up Time
This is the way we clean the room, clean the room,
   clean the room.
This is the way we clean the room, so early in the
   morning (or, before we go outside).

Snack or Meal Time
The more we get together, together, together.
The more we get together, the happier are we!

✳   Invite the children to turn traditional tales into musical
plays. "The Three Billy Goats Gruff" and "The Three Little Pigs"
both work well.

✳   Encourage sing-alongs. This is a good car activity. It's
also great at any family gathering, school meetings, or group
get-togethers.

Books for children

Lullabies and Night Songs by William Engvick
Froggie Went A-Courting by Chris Conover
I Like the Music by Leah Komaiko
Old MacDonald Had a Farm by Robert M. Quackenbush
Down by the Bay by Raffi
Wheels on the Bus by Raffi
"Bremen Town Musicians"—many versions available

Want to read more?

Begley, Sharon. 1996. "Your Child's Brain: How Kids are Wired
    for Music, Math and Emotions." Newsweek (February 19):
    55-58.
Clynes, Manfred. 1982. *Music, Mind and Brain.* New York:
    Plenum Press.
Graziano, Amy B., Gordon L. Shaw, and Eric L. Wright. 1997.
    "Music Training Enhances Spatial-Temporal Reasoning in
    Young Children: Towards Educational Experiments." *Early
    Childhood Connections* (Summer): 30-36.
Scartelli, Joseph P. 1984. "The Learning Brain." *Journal of Music
    Therapy* 21:67-78, 341.
Viadero, Debra. 1998. "Music on the Mind." *Education Week*:
    25-27.
Webb, Douglas, and Terry Webb. 1990. *Accelerated Learning
    with Music.* Norcross, GA: Accelerated Learning Systems.

The Power of New

Novelty and the Brain

The brain pays closer attention to things that don't fit an established pattern, things that are new and different (novel). What we are accustomed to becomes routine and, over time, the brain reacts to routine stimulus by lowering levels of stimulation. Anything new causes the body to release adrenaline, and adrenaline acts as a memory fixative. According to Arnold Scheibel, Director of the Brain Research Institute at UCLA, "Unfamiliar activities are the brain's best friend."

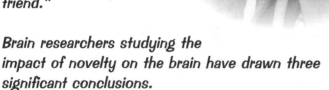

Brain researchers studying the impact of novelty on the brain have drawn three significant conclusions.
1. Rats in enriched environments grow brains with higher numbers of dendritic connections. Researchers believe that the same thing happens

when children are placed in enriched environments. This is tied to one of the key findings of recent research that states that early experiences contribute to brain structure and capacities.

2. Frequently changed environments (every two to four weeks) are needed to maintain increased dendrite connections. Again, researchers believe this is also true for human beings.

3. Real world experience provides one of the best environments for brain growth (see the chapters on sense and meaning and the brain, pages 112-115: problem solving, pages 97-104: and practice, pages 94-96).

Ideas for Using Novelty to Build Brain Power

✳ Rearrange children's toys and equipment every so often (about six weeks). Also rotate books on the library shelf. Note: Be sure children are ready for this; too much change can be upsetting.

✳ Rotate toys. Put some things away for a couple of months, then bring them out again.

✳ Rearrange the furniture. Let children help.

✳ Color on paper taped under a table or to a window.

✳ Cut easel paper into creative shapes.

✳ Try working backwards one day. Children really get a kick out of this, especially if you tie it to the book *Wacky Wednesday* by Theodore LeSieg.

✸   Create new verses to songs, and sing old ones to different tunes. Try singing "Itsy Bitsy Spider" (page 57) to the tune of "Twinkle, Twinkle, Little Star" (page 36) and vice versa.

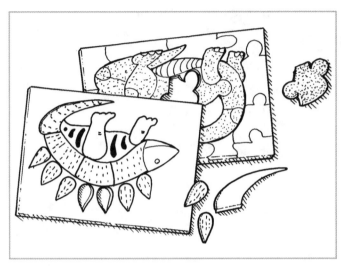

✸   Work puzzles upside down. String beads on strings that hang from the ceiling. Try riding tricycles or bicycles backwards.

✸   Place unusual items together. Try putting the dishes with the blocks or Legos with art supplies. Stand back and watch what happens.

✸   Try reading a book backwards. Sometimes it still makes sense. Try *Brown Bear, Brown Bear, What Do You See?* Try one that won't make sense.

✸   Have hot dogs for breakfast and pancakes for dinner.

✸   Eat snack or a meal outside or in another room. Make it a picnic.

✸   Switch roles. Let the children read to you, decide what to eat, or answer the phone all day.

✸   Encourage children to sleep at the opposite end of their beds.

✸   Take a walk in the neighborhood. Try walking backwards.

Ideas for Groups of Children

✳   Change names of traditional games. "Simon Says" can become "Chuckie Says," "Duck, Duck, Goose" can be "Dog, Dog, Cat."

✳   Make up new rules for games. Move backwards around a game board. Use a spinner/die combination instead of two dice.

✳   Rotate seating every few weeks. Sitting in the same seat each day has been proven to reduce alertness.

Books for children

Imogene's Antlers by David Small
Cat in the Hat by Dr. Seuss
Bored—Nothing to Do! by Peter Spier
Wacky Wednesday by Theo LeSieg
Look, Look Again by Tana Hoban
Jenny's Hat by Ezra Jack Keats
If... by Sarah Perry
Tuesday by David Wiesner
Falling Up by Shel Silverstein

Want to read more?

Scheibel, Arnold. 1994. "You Can Continuously Improve Your Mind and Your Memory." *Bottom Line Personal* (15) 21: 9-10.

Feeding the Brain

Nutrition and the Brain

Good nutrition is fundamental to brain function. Proteins (eggs, fish, tofu, chicken, yogurt) are critical to alertness, attention, and thinking. How much protein we need is dependent upon our age, weight, and activity levels. Typically, fifteen to thirty grams of protein per day is adequate.
Carbohydrates (breads, cereals, potatoes) slow down the alertness of the brain. In some studies, carbohydrates have been linked to aggressive behaviors. Low carbohydrate diets appear to lessen aggressive behaviors. Researchers have validated that sugar, especially when mixed with other carbohydrates, negatively affects attention span, focusing ability, and activity levels. However, sugar (when accompanied by protein) can have a positive influence on learning.

The brain seems to function best when diets include protein, carbohydrates with protein, selenium (seafood, nuts, whole-grain breads), boron (broccoli, apples, peaches, grapes), folic acid (green leafy vegetables, beef liver, beans), zinc (fish, beans, grains), and Vitamin B. All of these vitamins and nutrients are more effective when obtained from a natural source as opposed to a supplement.

Several studies have shown that cognitive functioning and behavior are enhanced by several small meals a day as opposed to our traditional three. Smaller, more frequent meals resulted in better insulin levels, lower cortisol levels, and better glucose tolerance.

Ideas for Using Nutrition to Build Brain Power

✳ Offer snacks that have low or no carbohydrates. Try instead protein-rich snacks such as cheese, yogurt, deviled eggs, nuts, and fruits.

✳ Teach about nutrition. Help children recognize healthy and unhealthy foods and habits.

✳ Set a good example. Eat healthy foods and talk about how they help you keep healthy.

✳ Try the following activities that allow children to tie food in with learning (check for food allergies beforehand):

> Read *Green Eggs and Ham* by Dr. Seuss, then fix green eggs and ham. Add green food coloring to the eggs before cooking; add margarine and green food coloring mixture to ham before cooking for a green glaze.

Invite children to shell peanuts. It's great for fine motor development. After they finish make peanut butter or just allow them to eat what they've shelled.

Dye eggs with natural dyes—purple (beet juice), yellow (tea), green (spinach or broccoli), pink (strawberries), and blue (blueberries). Boil items separately, reserving the liquid to use as the dyes. When the liquids are cooled, show the class which item produced which color. To reinforce dye concepts, let children dip strips of cloth into the liquid. After dyeing the eggs, invite the children to eat them.

Offer several types of nuts. Invite children to sort the nuts by picking them up with tongs and placing them into the compartments

of a muffin tin. After nuts are sorted, let everyone taste them. Ask children which was their favorite and graph the results.

Make letter pretzels.

1½ cups (360 ml) warm water
4 cups (1 L) wheat flour
1 envelope yeast
1 teaspoon salt
Mix all ingredients. Give each child enough dough to shape into the first letter of their names. Brush dough letters with beaten egg and sprinkle with coarse salt. Bake at 425°F (220°C) for 12 minutes.

Make finger gelatin shapes.

12 ounces (300 ml)
    frozen apple or
    grape juice
    (thawed)
3 envelopes of unfla-
    vored gelatin
1²/₃ cups (400 ml)
    hot water
Mix all ingredients.
    Stir well. Pour into
    a 9″ x 13″ (23 cm x
    33 cm) pan. Chill.
    Cut into shapes or
    strips.

✸   Try your own experiment. Provide nibbling items
throughout the day. Do you notice any differences in children's
level of alertness?

✸   Plan weekly menus with children. Discuss healthy
choices.

✸   Offer healthy snacks in the car such as carrot sticks,
fruit, and wheat crackers. They are all easy to eat in the car.

✸   Be sure children eat
breakfast; it starts the brain
working. Stay away from
carbohydrates. Encourage
eggs, yogurt, fruits, whole-
grain cereals, and breads.

Ideas for Groups of Children

✴ Create an open snack table. Regulate the number of times a child goes to the snack table by using a monitoring system. Try using key tags on a board with cup hooks. Color a happy face on one side and place the child's name on the other side. After the child has snacked, he can turn the key tag over so the happy face is showing. Clothespins with children's names on them could also be used to keep track of visits to the snack table.

Books for children

Green Eggs and Ham by Dr. Seuss
D.W. The Picky Eater by Marc Brown
Daddy Makes the Best Spaghetti by Anna Grossnickle Hines
Now I Will Never Leave the Dinner Table by Jane Read Martin
    and Patrick Mark
Growing Vegetable Soup by Lois Ehlert

Want to read more?

Connors, Keith. 1989. *Feeding the Brain; How Foods Affect Children*. New York: Plenum Press.
Wurtman, Richard. J. 1986. *Managing Your Mind and Mood through Food*. New York: HarperCollins.

More than Plaids

Patterns and the Brain

The brain thrives on making and detecting patterns. The human brain is not organized or designed for linear, one-path thought but instead operates by going down many paths simultaneously. It compiles information from many sources to determine size, shape, color, texture, weight, smell, movement, and so forth. The brain is constantly making sense out of many bits of information. During the process of making sense of data, the brain is in a state of confusion. When sense and meaning are established, the brain is ready for more challenges. Every pattern that the brain is able to create means that it can then store that new understanding to a nonconscious level of knowledge.

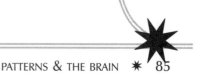

It is believed that the ability the see patterns and make relationships of the patterns is the essence of intelligence (see page 85). Helping children to see patterns in language, logic, behaviors, habits, music, body movements, nature, and space may be one of the most important aspect of what we teach.

Ideas for Using Patterns to Build Brain Power

✷ Look for visual patterns in the environment like shadows on the floor, lines in the carpet, window arrangement in buildings, and so on. Does the vacuum cleaner create a pattern on the rug? Does the lawn mower create a pattern on the grass? Is there a common cause to each pattern? Point out the patterns to children and encourage them to look for patterns on their own.

✷ Make sure children have many experiences that teach likenesses and differences. This understanding is critical to their ability to understand patterns.

✷ Read books and stories that have a repetitive pattern in the language of the text such as *Brown Bear, Brown Bear What Do You See?* by Bill Martin and "The Three Little Pigs."

✳   Read stories that have a repetitive pattern in the action like "The Three Billy Goats Gruff" and "The Gingerbread Man."

✳   Find patterns in numbers such as odd and even, counting by twos, fives, tens, or adding on one.

✳   Sing songs that have a pattern such as "The Green Grass Grew All Around, All Around," "She'll Be Comin' 'Round the Mountain," "This Old Man," and "Head, Shoulders, Knees, and Toes." Encourage children to make up new songs with a pattern.

"The Green Grass Grew All Around"
In the park there was a hole,
Oh, the prettiest hole you ever did see.
A hole in the park,
A hole in the ground,
And the green grass grew all around, all around,
And the green grass grew all around.

And in that hole there was a sprout,
Oh, the prettiest sprout you ever did see.
Sprout in the hole,
Hole in the ground,
And the green grass grew all around, all around,
And the green grass grew all around.

And from that sprout there grew a tree,
Oh, the prettiest tree you ever did see.
Tree from a sprout,
Sprout in a hole,
Hole in the ground,
And the green grass grew all around, all around,
And the green grass grew all around.

And on that tree there was a branch,
Oh, the prettiest branch you ever did see.
Branch on a tree,
Tree from a sprout,
Sprout in a hole,
Hole in the ground,
And the green grass grew all around, all around,
And the green grass grew all around.

And on that branch there was a nest,
Oh, the prettiest nest you ever did see.
Nest on a branch,
Branch on a tree,
Tree from a sprout,
Sprout in a hole,
Hole in the ground,
And the green grass grew all around, all around,
And the green grass grew all around.

And in that nest there was an egg,
Oh, the prettiest egg you ever did see.
Egg in a nest,
Nest on a branch,
Branch on a tree,
Tree from a sprout,
Sprout in a hole,
Hole in the ground,
And the green grass grew all around, all around,
And the green grass grew all around.

And in that egg there was a bird,
Oh, the prettiest bird you ever did see.
Bird in an egg,
Egg in a nest,
Nest on a branch,
Branch on a tree,
Tree from a sprout,
Sprout in a hole,
Hole in the ground,
And the green grass grew all around, all around,
And the green grass grew all around.

"This Old Man"

This old man, he played one,
He played knick-knack on my
    thumb.
With a knick-knack paddy-
    whack, give your dog a bone.
This old man came rolling home.

This old man, he played two,
He played knick-knack on my
    shoe.

Three—on my knee
Four—on my door
Five—on my hive
Six—on my sticks
Seven—up in heaven
Eight—on my gate
Nine—on my spine
Ten—once again

"Head, Shoulders, Knees and Toes"

Head, shoulders, knees and
    toes, knees and toes,
Head, shoulders, knees and
    toes, knees and toes,
And eyes and ears and mouth
    and nose.
Head, shoulders, knees and
    toes, knees and toes.

✳ Encourage children to
create patterns when painting.
For example, thin line/thick
line, red circle/blue circle,
line/dot, color/no color.

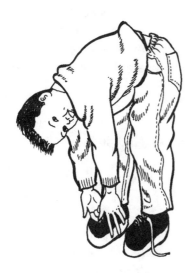

✳ Try weaving crepe paper into the sides of a plastic laundry
or milk crate, weaving construction paper mats, weaving in a
loom, or weaving crepe paper in a chain link fence. Point out
color patterns, space patterns, and the over/under movement
patterns.

✳ Make up simple dances with repetitive patterns.

✳ Listen to classical music and see if you can hear patterns in the music.

✳ Create clapping patterns. Let children record their patterns, then see if they can identify the one that they made up when they listen to the tape.

✳ Discuss the cyclical pattern of seasons, months of the year, and days of the week. Write the months of the year on paper plates. Arrange plates in a circle on the floor and invite children to walk around the circle as they recite the months.

✳ Talk about school days and weekend days. How are they alike? How are they different? What patterns occur in each type of day? How are the patterns alike? How are they different?

✳ Discuss the patterns of the body—the in and out motion of breathing, the rhythm of our heartbeat and pulse.

✳ Observe patterns in the weather. Can you use the patterns to predict weather?

✳ Cause and effect activities are based on patterns. Provide opportunities for children to explore cause and effect relationships. For example, encourage children to rub their hands together, sand a piece of wood, rub sticks together, or rub porous rocks together. What happens? Does it always happen that way?

✳ Play commercial games such as Simon or Bop-It.

✳ Provide a kaleidoscope. What creates the patterns? Make your own kaleidoscope.

✳ Try finding patterns in the tastes of foods. Which kinds of foods are sweet? Which are sour?

✳ Look for patterns in nature such as how the frost forms in crystals on the window-

pane, water rippling in a puddle, bark on a tree trunk, tree branches against the sky, where ferns grow, which side of the tree has moss, or the rhythm of the rain.

✳ Discuss routines. Help children see the repetitiveness of routines. For example, brushing teeth after meals, dance lessons every Wednesday, and trash pick-up on Mondays and Thursdays.

✳ Invite children to participate in pattern activities such as setting the table, putting away groceries, folding clothes, or cooking.

✳ Help children identify the patterns in clothing such as stripes, dots, and plaids.

Ideas for Groups of Children

✳ Provide children with four-inch (ten-centimeter) square sheets of colored cellophane. Invite them to go outside in the sunlight and create a pattern on the ground by letting the sun shine through the paper. Challenge them to make patterns. Suggest they combine their efforts with those of their friends.

✷   Watch for patterns in behaviors. Isn't it interesting that friends are more willing to share when you ask them nicely? Notice how everyone gets a little cranky around lunch time? How many people are tired after lunch?

✷   Play games with patterns such as Duck, Duck Goose, Hide and Seek, or Musical Chairs. Compare Musical Chairs with Cooperative Musical Chairs (see Multiple Intelligences, page 63). Challenge children to find the patterns. Where are the patterns different?

✷   Teach children simple dances like the "Bunny Hop" and "The Hokey Pokey." Both dances are made up of simple patterns and children will be able to identify the patterns and then physically move through the patterns. Square dancing is also made up of repetition of pattern movement.

"The Hokey Pokey"
(form a circle and act out the words)
You put your right foot in,
You put your right foot out,
You put your right foot in,
And you shake it all about.
You do the Hokey Pokey *(hold hands in the air and shake them)*
And you turn yourself around.
That's what it's all about.
Hey!
(Repeat, using other body parts.)

✷   Create patterns using the children. For example, one child faces forward, one backward, one forward, and so on. Challenge children to create new patterns.

✳ Use word maps. For example, if you are learning about sea life, let children tell you everything they know about it before you start. Write sea life on a chart tablet and draw a circle around it. Draw lines from the circle to note the information provided by the children.

Books for children

Goodnight Moon by Margaret Brown Wise
The Very Busy Spider by Eric Carle
Fortunately by Remy Charlip
The Doorbell Rang by Pat Hutchins
Jump, Frog, Jump by Robert Kalan
Brown Bear, Brown Bear, What Do You See? by Bill Martin Jr.
We're Going on a Bear Hunt by Michael Rosen
Caps for Sale by Esphyr Slobodkina
Have You Seen My Duckling? by Nancy Tafuri

Want to read more?

Caine, Renata N., and Geoffrey Caine. 1994. *Making Connections: Teaching the Human Brain.* Boston, MA: Addison-Wesley.

Coward, Andrew. 1990. *Pattern Thinking.* New York: Praeger Publishers.

Hart, Leslie. 1983. *Human Brain and Human Learning.* White Plains, NY: Longman Publishing.

Try, Try Again

Practice and the Brain

"Practice makes perfect" or does it? It is possible to repeat a skill over time and never improve. Think of people you know who, although they have been driving for years, have never improved their performance. If we practice without knowledge of what is necessary for improvement, no matter how much we practice, we will not get better.

According to David Sousa (1995), in order for practice to change our performance, three criteria must be met:

1. We must have all the knowledge necessary to understand the options available in applying the new knowledge or skill.

2. We must understand the steps in the process of applying the knowledge to deal with a particular situation.

3. We must be able to analyze the results of that application and know what variables need to be manipulated to improve performance in the future.

Practice improves a skill or helps individuals learn a concept only if it is monitored and feedback is provided. This kind of practice over time increases recall. According to research, we have only a ten percent chance of remembering something done once in thirty days, and a ninety percent chance of remembering something done six times in thirty days.

Ideas to Build Brain Power With Practice

✳   Offer information in small doses and increase the amount as children show understanding. For example, when learning to create patterns, introduce horizontal patterns created using two elements, such as buttons and crayons. Then move to more complex patterns by increasing the number of attributes and directions of patterns.

✳   As children gain confidence, arrange for older children to serve as tutors.

✳   Utilize peer teaching. Often children will more readily provide clear feedback to each other than adults. Children speak the same language and share perspectives.

✳ Teach the value of persistence and determination. "The Itsy Bitsy Spider" (page 57) provides a good example of try, try again. Many skills are mastered only after repeated failures and lots of trying again.

✳ When teaching children a skill, model the activity first. Teach in small chunks and add information as the children gain experience.

✳ Ask children to explain their thinking or how they are attempting to accomplish an activity. This provides insight for feedback.

✳ Offer feedback in a positive, helpful manner. Specific, supporting feedback helps perfect performance. If you ask children to explain their work to you, you will know what they understand and, therefore, what feedback will be specific and supportive.

✳ Help children feel good about the small improvements that will eventually result in accomplishment.

✳ Don't overload children's schedules. Too many activities leave no time for reflection. Reflection is critical to improvement. We all need time to reflect in order to evaluate and contemplate where we are and what's needed to become better at what we're doing.

Books for children

Whistle for Willie by Ezra Jack Keats
Itsy Bitsy Spider by Tracy Moncure, Pam Schiller (eds.)

Want to read more?

Sousa, David. 1995. *How the Brain Learns*. Reston, VA: The National Association of Secondary School Principals.

No Problem

Problem Solving and the Brain

Problem solving is one of the brain's favorite exercises. Problem solving causes synapses to form, chemicals to activate, and blood flow to increase. Researchers state that the brain only learns when it is confronted with a problem (placed in a state of confusion). When we encounter routine situations we simply repeat stored programs (already learned patterns). This is called replication of a habit and, according to researchers, it prohibits new learning. Problems force us to rethink our programs and patterns and, in so doing, the possibility for new learning emerges.

Supporting the notion that problems can create the opportunity for new learning, researchers state that when the learner is placed in a climate of suspense, surprise, and uncertainty, she can develop a richer understanding of content.

Problem solving naturally fuels our self-esteem. Think about how good you feel when you solve a problem.

Ideas to Build Brain Power With Problem Solving

✳   Teach the process of problem solving.
Step 1: Identify and articulate the problem.
Step 2: Brainstorm possible solutions.
Step 3: Evaluate possible solutions in terms of resources required.
Step 4: Select one of the solutions.
Step 5: Try it out.
Step 6: Evaluate the results. If first choice of solutions doesn't work, go back to Step 3 and try again.

✳   Problem solving generally means coming up with new or different ideas. Make sure children have plenty of different experiences.

✳   Read stories that are focused on problem solving such as *Stone Soup* by Marcia Brown, *Swimmy* by Leo Lionni, *The Three Billy Goats Gruff* by Paul Galdone, *Moira's Birthday* by Robert Munsch, and *Fish Out of Water* by Helen Palmer. Encourage children to evaluate the solutions. Can they think of other ways to solve the problem?

✳   Read stories that present problems. Stop after the problem has been identified and invite children to brainstorm solutions. *The Doorbell Rang* by Pat Hutchins is a good example of this type of story.

✳ Use a story, such as *Imogene's Antlers* by David Small, as a springboard to encourage children to write or dictate their own story with a problem and solution. Imogene wakes up with antlers on her head and spends the day solving the problems that come with a pair of antlers on one's head. At the end of the story, the antlers disappear but a new problem arises—a peacock tail. Children can use the story ending as a spark to begin their own story. *David's Father* by Robert Munsch is another good story for this type of activity.

✳ Ask questions that allow children to use higher level thinking skills. Take "The Three Billy Goats Gruff" for example. Some examples of questions that require higher level thinking are:

> Do you think it was okay for the smaller billy goat to tell the troll to wait for his bigger brother? Why or why not?
> How would the story be different if the troll were friendly?
> The troll used his ugly face to scare the goats. Can you think of other ways the troll could have frightened the goats?
> Which part of the story could happen in real life? Which parts are make believe?

✳ Provide opportunities for children to compare and contrast stories, activities, games, and concepts. Comparing and contrasting provide practice in scrutinizing possible solutions to problems. Try comparing two versions of "The Little Red Hen," or ask questions like "How is a bird different from a cat?"

✳ Ask "what if" questions. What if red were the only color? What if children were in charge of parents? What if horses could ride people? What if dogs could talk?

✳ Provide activities that require exercising judgment. For example, you might ask, "Do you think all of these marbles will fit in the jar?" or "Do you think it was all right for the Little Red Hen to refuse to share her bread?"

Try setting up activities that require problem solving:

Mix one cup (240 ml) of beans, one cup (240 ml) of salt, and one cup (240 ml) of rice together in a bowl. Provide the children with a strainer and a colander and tell them to separate the items in the bowl into three separate bowls—one with beans, one with salt, and one with rice. After the children are successful, ask them if they can think of another way to accomplish the task.

Show children five blocks of graduated sizes. Ask them to make a tower with the blocks. Encourage children to talk about the variety of ways they have built their towers, observing that there is more than one way to build a tower.

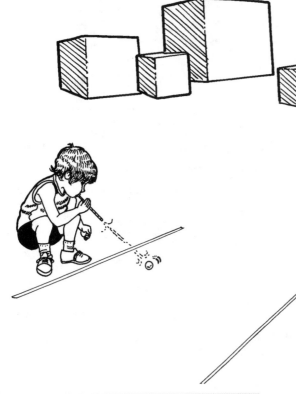

Place two long strips of masking tape on the floor, five feet (1.5 m) apart. Ask the children how they would move a Ping-Pong ball from one line to the other without touching it. (Some possibilities include blowing the ball through a straw, fanning it with a magazine or book, blowing on it with your mouth, or blowing it through a paper towel tube.)

Cut three to four sets of cat and bird tracks from black construction paper. Tape footprints on the floor with the bird prints perpendicular to the cat prints. The two sets of prints should meet at a right angle with only the cat prints continuing. Encourage the children to share their ideas of what happened. Children will guess things like the bird flew away, the cat ate the bird, and the bird hopped on the cat's back. Ask the children if there is any way they can know for sure what happened.

Fill a glass with pebbles and ask the children if the glass is full. If they say no, have them add pebbles until everyone agrees that the glass is full. Then ask if they think anything else will fit into the glass. The children will probably say no. Pour either salt or sand into the glass. The children will be surprised to see that the glass will hold more. Call their attention to how sand or salt fills in the spaces left between the pebbles. When you ask if the glass is full, the children will probably say yes again. Pour water into the glass. Children will be surprised. Ask if anybody knows why the glass could hold the water. Discuss the importance of evaluating what we hear; children may mistakenly concentrate on the pebbles instead of the question, "Is the glass full?"

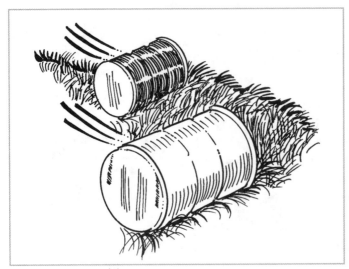

Give children two coffee cans and several smaller items to place inside the cans (e.g., a roll of tape, a small book, a crayon, a block). Encourage children to explore the way the item inside a can affects the way the can rolls. If children want to race their cans, use masking tape as the finish line.

✳ Model problem solving. Talk through problems and related decision making with children when appropriate.

✳ When child-sized problems occur, let children solve them. Don't solve problems for them; help them through the process. For example, when the juice is spilled, let the children experiment with several ways of cleaning it up (sponge, dish cloth, napkin, etc.).

✳ When children ask "why" questions, encourage them to think through the possible answers. For example, when the flashlight burns out, lead them to the conclusion that it might be the batteries instead of answering "It probably needs new batteries."

✳ Teach riddles and introduce brain teasers. These are great car activities. For example, try finding things that are a certain color, or when children get older, things that start with each letter of the alphabet.

✳ Use television programs as a platform for problem solving. Most story lines are developed around a problem/resolution. Discuss possible/probable solutions during commercials. Discuss programs after they are over. Did the characters do a good job solving the problem?

✳ Read chapter books that use a problem/resolution format such as *Mr. Popper's Penguins* by Richard and Florence Atwater, *A Toad for Tuesday* by Russell Erickson, or *Maurice's Room* by Paula Fox. Read one chapter each evening and discuss the problem or plot as it unfolds.

✳ Use discipline that includes children in the process of coming up with solutions. This type of discussion and use of natural or logical consequences is far more beneficial to children's development of self-control than adult handed-down punishment. For example, four-year-old Heather drags her feet every morning when getting ready to leave the house. Instead of her mother nagging her or punishing her, she sits down and asks Heather for suggestions that might be a solution to the problem. Between the two of them, they think of the following possibilities: Heather could get up earlier; she could lay out her clothes the night before; she could go to the child care center in her pajamas; she could use the timer on the stove to pace herself; or she could go to bed earlier so she won't be tired in the morning. Allowing Heather to help choose a solution will provide a much greater chance of changing the behavior.

✳ Recycle as much as possible. Explain that this is an individual solution to a global problem.

✳ Read the funny papers with your child. Many of the cartoons use a problem/solution format.

✳ Pose problems for children to attack. For example, how many ways can you think of to move the trash can from its storage spot to the curb for pick up?

✳ Select a child care center or school that supports allowing children to solve problems as part of their learning experience.

Ideas for Groups of Children

✳   Set up problem-focused scenarios and encourage the children to come up with solutions. For example, Richele and Sam are playing with Sam's new trucks. When Austin shows up to play there are three children but only two trucks. How many ways can you think of to involve Austin in the play (e.g., share the trucks, let Austin work the service station or loading dock, put the trucks away and play with something else)?

✳   Create puppet shows based on a problem and let the children act out various solutions.

Books for children

Imogene's Antlers by David Small
The Doorbell Rang by Pat Hutchins
David's Father by Robert Munsch
Stone Soup by Marcia Brown
The Little Red Hen by Paul Galdone
Moira's Birthday by Robert Munsch
Three Billy Goats Gruff by Paul Galdone
Swimmy by Leo Lionni
Mike Mulligan and His Steam Shovel by Virginia Lee Burton

Want to read more?

Cleick, James. 1987. *Making a New Science*. New York: Viking.
Doll, William. E., Jr. 1989. "Complexity in the Classroom." *Educational Leadership* 47.1: 65-70.
Howard, Pierce J. 1994. *The Owner's Manual for the Brain: Everyday Applications from Mind-Brain Research*. Austin, TX: Leornian Press.
Prigogine, Iyla, and Isabelle Stengers. 1984. *Order Out of Chaos*. New York: Bantam.

Praise or Encouragement

Rewards and Praise and the Brain

Rewards are often used to motivate children to behave in a certain way. Generally, rewards do encourage predictable behavior but, in the long run, may kill the intrinsic joy of learning. Children who are bribed for good work or good behavior soon tire of the designated reward and begin to require a bigger and better reward. They learn to "work the system." All the while they are not learning the internal joy that is part of accomplishment. Some studies even suggest that excessive praise can cause children to develop performance anxiety. In one study, students who were praised prior to taking a skills test performed worse than students who did not receive praise. Research suggests that "extrinsic motivation inhibits intrinsic motivation." A reward system prevents the establishment of intrinsic motivation because there's

rarely an incentive to be creative—only to do the requested behavior.

Replace rewards with positive alternatives. Try modeling the joy of learning; increasing specific feedback; and offering choices, peer support, and self-assessment. When was the last time your boss stopped in to tell you what a good job you were doing or to offer you a bonus for doing your job?

Ideas to Build Brain Power Without Praise and Rewards

✳ Reduce the amount of praise you provide; replace it with feedback. For example, instead of, "That's a great painting, Tiffany," you might say, "The red and yellow colors you used for the trees help create a fall look to your painting, Tiffany."

✳ Use encouragement instead of praise. For example, "I can tell you put a lot of effort into your drawing, Brandon."

✳ Help children learn to evaluate their own efforts. Let them critique themselves.

✳ Focus on process as opposed to product. For example, instead of saying, "Your building turned out great, Ginny," say, "Gee, Ginny, that building shows a lot of hard work you did all by yourself."

✳ Be careful not to set children up for failure. For example, if you say, "Gabrielle, you are always so nice," you leave her open to failure. No one is nice all the time.

✳ Use a natural voice when offering support to children. Be specific and sincere. Children recognize and generally ignore stock phrases such as, "good job," "terrific work," and "very good."

✳ Invite children to select their own rewards.

✳ Allow children to have more choices. Choices increase intrinsic motivation.

✳ Encourage children's progress by making accurate statements of improvement; for example, "Steve, you set the table with all the silverware today."

✳ Be supportive of the processes children use instead of only commenting on the finished products. For example, "I noticed you spent a lot of time looking for just the right colors for your picture, Rosie," instead of "Rosie, your picture looks terrific." Encouraging effort helps children focus on the most meaningful part of the activity and encourages the transfer of effort to the next task.

✳ Avoid promising concrete rewards for appropriate behaviors. Instead, help children feel good about their appropriate behaviors. Remember, children earn and lose privileges. We are all entitled to food, shelter, safety, and education. Everything else is a privilege that is earned and can be lost when behavior warrants.

✳ Use allowance as a way of teaching fiscal responsibility—not as a reward.

✳ Share success stories. Let your pride show.

Ideas for Groups of Children

✳ Eliminate the use of stickers and privilege rewards. Help children learn to accept the completion of task and accomplishment of goals as rewards in and of themselves.

✳ Avoid comparisons and competitions. "I like the way Linda is sitting," puts Linda in competition with her friends. It also demoralizes others who were sitting quietly but were not recognized. It is always better to provide children feedback on their individual progress. For example, "Phillip, you are improving at matching letters to sounds."

Books for children

Whistle for Willie by Ezra Jack Keats
Amazing Grace by Mary Hoffman
Dance, Tanya by Patricia Lee Gauch
The Little Red Hen by Paul Galdone

Want to read more?

Amabile, Teresa. 1989. *Growing Up Creative*. New York: Crown Publishing.

Hitz, Randy, and Amy Driscoll. 1988. "Praise or Encouragement? New Insights into Praise: Implications for Early Childhood Teachers." *Young Children*. Washington, DC: NAEYC.

Kohn, Alfie. 1993. *Punished by Rewards*. New York: Houghton-Mifflin.

Zimmerman, Barry, Sebastian Bonner and Robert Kovach. 1996. *Developing Self-Regulated Learners: Beyond Achievement to Self-Efficacy*. Washington DC: American Psychology Association.

Spanish, Chinese, Arabic

Learning a Second Language and the Brain

Between the fourth and eighth months of life, the brain assigns a neuron to every sound in a child's native language. The neurons are connected and strengthened as the child begins to connect sounds and speech. If more than one language is heard, neurons are assigned to the second language as well.

During the early years a child's brain is highly receptive to language. Some researchers suggest teaching children—especially those from birth to six—fifty words of a second language. This allows the brain to assign neurons to the sounds of the language. It appears that the brain's affinity for language remains active up to the approximate age of ten, so formal instruction can be offered between six *and ten. The result should be a child who speaks a second language without dialect or accent, and without having to mentally translate from one language to the other. After ten years of age a child can certainly still learn a second language, but the task will become increasingly difficult and the chance of speaking the second language without an accent, dialect, or translation is unlikely.*

Ideas to Build Brain Power With a Second Language

✳ If you speak a second language, take ten to twenty minutes a day to teach it to children in an organized fashion.

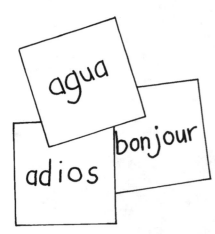

✳ Even if you don't speak a second language, teach simple words in another language such as numbers, colors, family members' names, days of the week, and months of the year. For example, *agua* for water, *adios* for good-bye, and *bonjour* for good morning.

✳ Show videos in a foreign language. They are available in most video stores. It might be fun to watch it first in English, then in another language.

✳ Solicit help from a senior citizen who speaks another language. A high school student would also be a good role model.

✳ Watch television on a station that provides programming in a foreign language.

✳ Encourage children to play with children who speak another language.

✳   Go to fairs that focus on different cultures so children will hear people speak another language. If you live in a culturally rich area, bring children to restaurants, stores, and gathering places where people speak another language. If possible, take trips to countries where they speak a language different from your native language. Challenge the whole family to try to speak the foreign language.

✳   Play songs with lyrics in foreign languages.

✳   If you know a child who is bilingual, ask her to help teach children a second language.

Books for children

Abuela by Arthur Dorros
Madeleine by Ludwig Bemelmans
A Chance for Esperanza by Pam Schiller and Alma Flor Ada
The Park Bench by Fumiko Takeshita
Bread Is for Eating by David and Phyllis Gershator
Emeka's Gift by Ifeoma Onyefulu

Want to read more?

Chugani, Harry T. 1991. "Imaging Human Brain Development with Position Emission Tomography." *Journal of Nuclear Medicine* 32.1: 23-26.

Dhority, Lynn. 1992. *The ACT Approach. The Use of Suggestion for Integrative Learning.* Philadelphia, PA: Gordon and Breach Science Publishers.

Kotulak, Ronald. 1993. "Unraveling Hidden Mysteries of the Brain." *Chicago Tribune* (April): 11-16.

Rose, Colin Penfield. 1997. *Accelerated Learning into the 21st Century: The Six-Step Plan to Unlock Your Master-Mind.* New York: Doubleday.

What Does It Mean?

Sense and Meaning in the Brain

Getting information transferred to long-term memory is critical since we can't remember what has not been stored. For information to be stored in our long-term memory, two criteria need to be met. First, the information must make sense, and, second, it must have meaning.

"Sense" means that the learner can fit the information into existing understanding. "Meaning" means the information is regarded as relevant to the learner. It is possible for something to make sense to us but be of little relevance. For example, it makes sense that football players practice thirty hours a week during football season, but unless you are a football player or a die-hard fan, the information is not relevant to your

daily life. The chances of your brain storing that information are slim (unless you're a trivia buff).

Meaning is more significant. Many things make sense to us (e.g., movies, books we read, conversations we have, things we see at the mall), but we don't keep the memory of all these things in permanent storage. Have you ever gone to a movie and not been able to even remember the plot a few weeks later? If the movie has meaning because it is a movie about teachers and you are a teacher, you have a far greater chance of remembering not only the plot, but details as well.

Ideas to Build Brain Power With Sense and Meaning

✳ Ask questions that allow children to match new information to what they have experienced. For example, if you read "The Three Billy Goats Gruff," you might ask children if they can think of a time when they were frightened like the small- and medium-sized goats were, or ask them if they could be one of the characters, which one would they choose? These kinds of questions help children make the story meaningful for them.

✳ Ask questions that allow you to assess children's understanding at the beginning, middle, and end.

✳ Invite children to think of ways they will apply what they are learning. List their answers on paper or chalkboard.

✳ Present the big picture first. Too many times we start with the part and build to the whole. Sense and meaning are easier to accomplish if children see the whole first. For example, with letter recognition and sounds, start by pointing out words in written text and then the letters within the words.

Invite children to write their names on six- by four-inch (fifteen-by ten-centimeter) pieces of poster board and then cut the letters apart to make name puzzles. Working the puzzles allows children to put the part/whole relationship of letters and words in perspective.

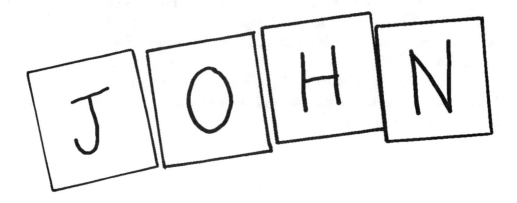

✳ Follow the interests of children by listening to the questions they ask and watching the choices they make. Teaching manners is far easier within the context of children playing with their peers than when presented piecemeal or outside of any context. How many times have you been driving somewhere and decided the unfilled time seemed like a good time to offer appropriate behavior tips to a child? The time might be right for you but certainly out of context to the child.

✳ Try to make sure children understand how they can use information you are wanting them to hear. Instead of telling children they need to learn to read so that they can do math and science projects, tell them that when they learn to read they can do their own ordering from menus when you're dining out. Introduce content with a "What's in it for me?" connection. Help children understand from the beginning how the information will benefit them. For example, if you are teaching one-to-one correspondence, tell children a story about how other children used the skill to pass out supplies or set the table for snack.

✳   Make home-school connections. For example, if children are learning about insects at school, invite them to help dig a garden at home. Find and point out the various insects you see. If children are learning matching at school, let them help you put the groceries away. They'll have fun applying their ability to match like items.

✳   When providing information to children, check for understanding along the way. If you wait until you've delivered the whole message you may be too late.

✳   Ask children how they will apply what they have learned. Questions such as "What have you learned?" or "What will you do with what you have learned?" are two examples. If Sage just hit his brother Steve, ask him how he will handle the situation next time. This helps children make sense and understand the relevance of what they've learned, and, therefore, remember it. According to research, we remember twenty percent of what we read, thirty percent of what we hear, fifty percent of what we read and hear, seventy percent of what we say, and ninety percent of what we say and do.

Books for children

The Holes in Your Nose by Genichiro Yagyu
Here Are My Hands by Bill Martin Jr.
Leo the Late Bloomer by Robert Kraus
Apples and Pumpkins by Anne Rockwell
The Kissing Hand by Audrey Penn
Something Special by Nicola Moon

Want to read more?

Kotulak, Ronald. 1997. *Inside the Brain: Revolutionary Discoveries of How the Mind Works*. Kansas City, MO: Andrews and McMeel.
Sousa, David. 1995. *How the Brain Learns*. Reston, VA: The National Association of Secondary School Principals.

The Hand-Brain Connection

Small Muscles and the Brain

Using the fingers not only stimulates the hands, it also stimulates the brain. Studies have confirmed that stimulation of the whole or parts of the body can stimulate the brain. Laboratory animals that were allowed to work with manipulatives for an hour a day for three months showed an increase in both size and connections in the brain. Many researchers have validated the positive effects of tactile stimulation (touching textured materials). In fact, researchers tell us we need to manipulate our fingers as we grow older if we want to stay mentally alert. There has never been a concert pianist who had problems with senility. The brain activates our hands and feet, and it appears that the reverse is also true.

Ideas to Build Brain Power
With Small Muscles

 Do fingerplays every day.

"Open, Shut Them"
Open, shut them, open, shut them,
Give a little clap.
Open, shut them, open, shut them,
Put them in your lap.

Creep them, creep them, creep
   them, creep them,
Right up to your chin.
Open wide your smiling mouth,
But do not let them in.

Creep them, creep them, creep
   them, creep them,
Past your cheeks and chin,
Open wide your smiling eyes,
Peeking in—Boo!

Creep them, creep them, creep them, creep them,
Right down to your toes.
Let them fly up in the air and
Bop you on the nose!

Open, shut them, open, shut them,
Give a little clap.
Open, shut them, open, shut them,
Put them in your lap.

"Ten Little Fingers"
I have ten little fingers,
And they all belong to me,
I can make them do things.
Would you like to see?

I can shut them up tight,
Or open them wide,
I can put them together,
Or make them all hide.
I can make them jump high,
Or make them go low.
I can fold them up quietly,
And sit just so.

✻ Use clapping and dancing activities. For example, "Who Stole the Cookie from the Cookie Jar," "Miss Mary Mack," "If You're Happy and You Know It" (see page 35), "Here We Go Round the Mulberry Bush," and "Hello! My Name Is Joe!" are all great action songs.

"Who Stole the Cookie from the Cookie Jar"
Who stole the cookie from the cookie jar?
(Name) stole the cookie from the cookie jar.
Who, me?
Yes, you.
Couldn't be.
Then who?
(New name chosen by the first accused) stole the cookie from the cookie jar.
Who, me?
Yes, you.
Couldn't be.
Then who?

Say this chant as you pat your thighs then snap in a rhythmic motion. Continue until everyone has been "accused" at least once.

COOKIES

"Miss Mary Mack"

Miss Mary Mack, Mack, Mack
All dressed in black, black, black
With silver buttons, buttons, buttons
All down her back, back, back.
She asked her mother, mother, mother
For fifteen cents, cents, cents
To see the elephants, elephants, elephants
Jump over the fence, fence, fence.
They jumped so high, high, high
They touched the sky, sky, sky
And they never came down, down, down
'Til the Fourth of July, ly, ly,
And they never came down, down, down
'Til the Fourth of July.

"Hello! My Name Is Joe!"

Hello! My name is Joe!
I have a wife, one kid and I work in a button
    factory.
One day, my boss said, "Are you busy?"
I said, "No."
"Then turn a button with your right hand." *(make turning
    gesture with right hand)*

Hello! My name is Joe!
I have a wife, two kids and I work in a button factory.
One day, my boss said, "Are you busy?"
I said, "No."
"Then turn a button with your left hand."
    *(make turning gesture with left hand
    as you continue with the right hand)*

*Continue adding number of children and
adding right and left feet and head.*

Hello! My name is Joe!
I have a wife, six kids and I work in a
    button factory.
One day, my boss said, "Are you busy?"
I said, "Yes!"

✳ Encourage children to do puzzles, put together tinker toys, or use lacing boards and pegboards. All these activities exercise small muscles. Create homemade puzzles by cutting up greeting cards or fronts of cereal boxes.

✳ Encourage children to collect small items on nature walks. Turn a piece of masking tape inside out to make a bracelet or belt to hold the collected items.

✳ Encourage water play activities to exercise the small muscles such as using eyedroppers, sponges, or basters to transfer water. A bar of soap provides both a nice tactile activity and an opportunity to work small muscles.

✳ Invite children to use tweezers or clothespins to pick up small items such as buttons or seeds and transfer them from one location to another.

✳ Do finger painting. Add sand or salt to the paints to encourage more exploration. Shaving cream makes a great finger paint on snowy days.

✳ Fill spray bottles with liquid tempera paint and extra water. Attach a large sheet of butcher paper on a wall or outside on a fence. Invite children to spray a design or a picture on the paper. This activity works best outdoors.

✳ Provide paper and invite children to tear it into various shapes. Invite them to glue their shapes to another piece of paper to create pictures.

✳ Make Gak or Goop. Encourage children to squeeze, roll, pat, and create with it.

Gak
2 cups (480 ml) glue
1½ (360 ml) cups tap water
2 teaspoons borax
1 cup (240 ml) hot water
food coloring
measuring cups and spoons

small and large mixing bowls
mixing spoons
tray

Combine glue, tap water, and food coloring in a bowl. In a larger bowl, dissolve the borax in the hot water. Slowly add the glue mixture. It will thicken quickly and be difficult to mix. Mix well and drain off excess water. Let stand for a few minutes, then pour into a tray. Let dry for ten minutes. Store in resealable plastic bags. It will keep two to three weeks.

Goop

2 cups (480 ml) salt
1 cup (240 ml) water
1 cup (240 ml) cornstarch
measuring cups
saucepan
stove or hot plate

Cook salt and ½ cup (120 ml) of water 4-5 minutes. Remove from heat. Add cornstarch and ½ cup (120 ml) water. Return to heat. Stir until mixture thickens. Store in plastic bag or covered container.

✳ Provide playdough with pipe cleaners, buttons, and cookie cutters to encourage working the finger muscles.

✸   Try origami, the Japanese art of paper folding. There are several excellent books available with simple directions.

✸   Teach string tricks like "The Winking Eye" and "Cup and Saucer" (see illustrations).

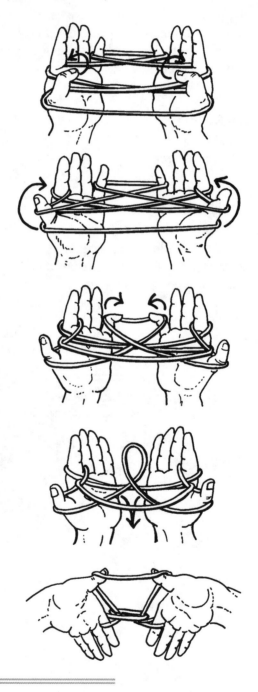

✳ Encourage children to use a typewriter. It's a great way to teach letter recognition and develop small muscles at the same time.

✳ Provide children with a pastry brush, scoop, and sand. Invite them to use the brush to sweep the sand into the scoop and dump it into a container.

✳ Shell peas or peanuts. Both work small muscles. Make peanut butter or pea soup afterwards.

✳ Try eating with chopsticks. It can be a challenging experience for the whole family.

✳ Bake bread and encourage children to help knead the dough.

✳ Invite children to help prepare snacks and meals. They can peel potatoes or carrots, shell peas, break up lettuce, wash fruits and vegetables, cut up vegetables (provide a plastic knife for young children), and help measure. Cleaning up after dinner provides

great opportunities to exercise fingers when using a sponge for cleaning off the table or washing dishes.

✳ Teach children how to tie their shoes. When they are older teach them how to crochet or sew on buttons.

✳ Offer music lessons. Playing a piano, guitar, violin, or flute requires using the fingers.

✸ Encourage children to help fold clothes and put away silverware. Dusting is also good for small muscle use.

Ideas for Groups of Children

✸ Encourage children to play games like Jacks, Pick-Up Sticks, Marbles, Dominoes, Tiddly Winks, and Drop the Clothespin.

✸ Play Hot Potato. Pass a beanbag around the circle while music is playing. When the music stops, the child with the beanbag is out of the game. Continue until only one child is left. Invite children who are out of the game to clap as the bag is passed.

Books for children

Here Are My Hands by Bill Martin Jr. and John Archambault
A Painter by Douglas Florian
The Paper Crane by Molly Bang
Hand, Hand, Fingers, Thumb by Al Perkins
Hand Rhymes by Marc Brown
Finger Rhymes by Marc Brown
Cleversticks by Bernard Ashley

Want to read more?

Dartigues, Jean-Francois. 1994. "Use It or Lose It." *Omni* (February): 34.
Houston, Jean. 1982. *The Possible Human: A Course in Enhancing Your Physical, Mental and Creative Abilities.* Los Angeles, CA: Jeremy Tarcher.

Appendices and Index

Glossary

Amygdala—A structure in the limbic region of the brain that encodes emotional messages to the hippocampus.

Axon—A long fiber that carries impulses from one neuron to the dendrites of other neurons.

Brain stem—A sea horse-shaped part of the brain that receives sensory input from eleven of the body's twelve nerve endings. The brain stem also monitors our heartbeat, body temperature, and digestion.

Cerebellum—The part of the brain located at the base of the skull. It is responsible for muscle coordination and movement.

Cerebrum—The largest part of the brain. It controls speech, memory, sensory interpretation, and thinking.

Dendrite—The branched formations from a neuron that receive impulses from other neurons through synaptic contact.

EEG—An instrument that charts fluctuations in the brain's electrical activity.

Glial cells—Brain cells that surround each neuron for support, protection, and nourishment.

Hippocampus—The part of the brain that compares new learning to past learning and encodes information to long-term memory.

Limbic system—The portion of the brain that includes the hippocampus and amygdala and controls emotions.

MRI—Magnetic Resonance Imaging. An instrument that uses radio waves to produce high contrast images of internal structures.

Neuron—The basic cell making up the brain and nervous system.

Neurotransmitter—Chemicals stored in an axon sac that are responsible for transmitting impulses from neuron to neuron across synaptic gaps.

Perceptual register—A structure in the brain stem that filters incoming stimuli before it is passed to working memory.

PET—Positron Emmision Tomography. A scanner that traces the metabolism of radioactively tagged sugar in the brain tissue to produce imagery of cell activity.

Retention—The preservation of information in long-term memory.

RAS—Reticular Activating System. A formation of neurons in the brain stem that channel sensory information through the perceptual register.

Short term memory—A temporary memory where information is processed briefly and unconsciously before being blocked or passed to working memory.

Synapse—A microscopic gap between the axon of one neuron and the dendrite of another.

Brain Fast Facts

✳ Researchers have determined that some memories actually do exist physically in the brain. When behaviors are repeated numerous times the brain forms a physical manifestation of the behavior called a biological substrate. If there is a behavior we want to see automatic in young children, repetition is the key.

✳ Neurons for vision begin forming between the second and fourth month of life. By the time children are two, the synapses in the human brain that allow sight have matured. Provide plenty of visually stimulating activities for infants.

✳ The optimum time for music instruction is between the ages of three and ten. There are few examples of professional musicians who began studying music later in life. As an added benefit, researchers believe that music affects spatial-temporal reasoning (the ability to see part/whole relationships). Children who take piano lessons at the age of three or four score higher on this reasoning skill than their peers who did not receive music instruction.

✳ Emotions boost memory. When emotions are engaged, the brain is activated. Emotions create a release of chemicals that act as a memory fixative. We all remember our "lowest" lows and our "highest" highs. Engage emotions; get children involved and excited.

✳ Small muscle exercise stimulates brain growth. Researchers have verified the positive effects of digital manipulation on the brain. Keep those stringing beads, pegs, and clay available.

✳ The size of a toddler's vocabulary is strongly correlated to how much a mother talks to the child. Talk to children about everything: what they are wearing, what you are doing, what lunch looks like, tastes like, and so on. The more words they hear, the more words they will say.

✳ Infants form permanent maps in their brains based on the native language they hear. During the first year of life, infants distinguish the phonemes (smallest units of sound) of the language they hear, and neurons in their brains are responsible for sorting out different sounds. After the first year of life it becomes increasingly difficult for a child to distinguish between sounds. Talk, talk, talk!

✳ Touching babies increases digestive abilities and decreases stress. Infants and toddlers will be calmer when babies digest their food easily and are free from stress. It's time for the good old rocking chair and lap holding. A pat on the back and a hug count, too.

Reprinted with permission from
Child Care Information Exchange, P.O. Box 2890, Redmond, WA 98073,
1-800-221-2864

Brain Research Facts Related to Memory and Retention

Emotions enhance memory. Events that are accompanied by intense emotion are more easily recalled. Think of a year; then think of an event that occurred in your life that year. Was an emotion attached to that memory?

Diet activates memory. Proteins are needed to convert stimuli from the external world to electrical signals within the brain (Jensen, 1995). We all need twenty to thirty grams of protein each day.

The more connections made between the information being learned and existing patterns in the brain, the greater the chances of moving information from working memory to long-term memory. For example, when studying zoo animals you might want to take a field trip, read a book, shape animals from clay, classify the animals, make up zoo stories, and role play the field trip or book.

Learning about something in meaningful context increases memory. Meaningful context requires that the material being presented is relevant and that the learner can make connections between the material and information he or she already understands or sees a need to understand.

Novelty can boost memory. Our bodies release chemicals when under stress. Positive stress increases adrenaline and negative stress increases cortisol. Both chemicals act as memory fixatives. Novelty creates positive stress. When a situation is different from existing patterns, the learner is challenged.

We remember the first and last of a lesson better than the middle. Psychologists call this the BEM—beginning, end, middle—principal. It is better to offer short episodes of learning where there are more beginnings and ends and fewer middles.

Memory is more accurately kept by revisiting the information frequently. Each time a learner reviews information, variables change (e.g., the context, the listener, the age of the learner).

Practice makes permanent. When a learner practices what has been learned over a period of time, retention is increased. For example, remembering a dance is easier when we practice it over a period of time as opposed to practicing it many times in one day.

References

Amabile, Teresa. 1989. *Growing Up Creative*. New York: Crown Publishers.

Armstrong, Thomas. 1993. *Seven Kinds of Smart: Identifying and Developing Your Many Intelligences*. Alexandria, VA: Association for Supervision and Curriculum Development.

Armstrong, Thomas. 1994. *Multiple Intelligences in the Classroom*. Alexandria, VA: Association for Supervision and Curriculum Development.

Baumeister, Roy. 1984. "Choking Under Pressure: Self-Consciousness and Paradoxical Effects of Incentives on Skillful Performance." *Journal of Personality and Social Psychology* 46: 610-20.

Begley, Sharon. 1997. "How to Build a Baby's Brain," *Newsweek* (Spring/Summer Special Edition): 28-32.

Begley, Sharon. 1996. "Your Child's Brain: How Kids Are Wired for Music, Math and Emotions." *Newsweek*. (February 19): 55-58.

Birren, Faber. 1997. *Color and Human Resources*. New York: Wiley.

Brierley, John Keith. 1994. *Give Me a Child Until He Is Seven: Brain Studies and Early Childhood Education*. Bristol, PA: Falmer Press.

Brown, John. S., and K. VanLehn. 1980. "Repair Theory: A Generative Theory of Bugs in Procedural Skills." *Cognitive Science* 4: 379-426.

Caine, Renata Nummela, and Geoffrey Caine. 1994. *Making Connections: Teaching the Human Brain*. Boston, MA: Addison-Wesley.

Cambell, Don G., and Chris B. Brewer. 1991. *Rhythms of Learning: Creative Tools for Developing Lifelong Skills.* Tucson, AZ: Zephyr Press.

Chugani, Harry T. 1991. "Imaging Human Brain Development with Position Emission Tomography." *Journal of Nuclear Medicine* 32.1: 23-26.

Clark, David L. Jeffrey Kreutzberg, and Francis K. W. Chee. 1977. "Vestibular Stimulation Influence on Motor Development in Infants." *Science* 196: 1228-1229.

Cleik, James. 1987. *Chaos: Making a New Science.* New York: Viking.

Clynes, Manfred. 1982. *Music, Mind and Brain.* New York: Plenum Press.

Connors, Keith. 1989. *Feeding the Brain: How Foods Affect Children.* New York: Plenum Press.

Cousins, Norman. 1989. *Head First: The Biology of Hope.* New York: Dutton.

Coward, Andrew. 1990. *Pattern Thinking.* New York: Praeger Publishers.

Dartigues, Jean F. 1994. "Use It or Lose It." *Omni* (February): 34.

Davis, Joel. 1997. *Mapping the Mind: The Secrets of the Human Brain and How It Works.* Secausus, NJ: Birch Lane Press.

Deci, Edward, and Richard M. Ryan. 1985. *Intrinsic Motivation and Self Determination in Human Behavior.* New York: Plenum.

Dennison, Paul, and Gail Dennison. 1988. *Brain Gym.* Teacher's Ed. Ventura, CA: Edu-kinesthetics.

Dienstbier, Richard A. 1989. "Periodic Adrenalin Arousal Boosts Health, Coping." *Brain-mind Bulletin*, 14.9A.

Dhority, Lynn. 1992. *The ACT Approach. The Use of Suggestion for Integrative Learning*. Philadelphia, PA: Gordon & Breach Science Publishers.

Doll, William E. Jr. 1989. "Complexity in the Classroom." *Educational Leadership* 47.1:65-70.

Dumas, Lynne S. 1998. "IQ vs. EQ: Brains Aren't Everything." *Parents Magazine* 73: 140.

Families and Work Institute. 1996. "Rethinking the Brain: New Insights into Early Development." Executive summary of the Conference on Brain Development in Young Children: New Frontiers for Research, Policy, and Practice, University of Chicago, June.

Fry, William F. Jr. And Walleed A. Salanch. 1993. *Advances in Humor and Psychotherapy*. Sarasota, FL: Professional Resource Exchange, Inc.

Gardner, Howard. 1983. *Frames of Mind: The Theory of Multiple Intelligences*. New York: Basic Books.

Glasser, William, and Karen Dotson. 1998. *Choice Theory in the Classroom*. New York: Harpercollins.

Goleman, Daniel. 1995. *Emotional Intelligence*. New York: Bantam.

Graziano, Amy B., Gordon L. Shaw and Eric L. Wright. 1997. "Music Training Enhances Spatial-Temporal Reasoning in Young Children: Towards Educational Experiments." *Early Childhood Connections* (Summer): 30-36.

Handcock, LynNell, and Pat Wingert. 1997. "The New Preschool." 129 *Newsweek* (Spring/Summer Special Edition): 36-37.

Hart, Leslie. 1983. *Human Brain and Human Learning*. White Plains, NY: Longman Publishing.

Hitz, Randy, and Amy Driscoll. 1988. "Praise or Encouragement? New Insights into Praise: Implications for Early Childhood Teachers." *Young Children*. Washington, DC: NAEYC.

Houston, Jean. 1982. *The Possible Human: A Course in Enhancing Your Physical, Mental and Creative Abilities*. Los Angeles, CA: Jeremy Tarcher, 333.

Howard, Pierce J. 1994. *The Owner's Manual for the Brain: Everyday Applications from Mind-Brain Research*. Austin, TX: Leornian press.

Jensen, Eric. 1994. *Brain-Based Learning*. Del Mar, CA. Turning Point Publishing.

Klein, Raymond, and Roseanne Armitage. 1979. "Brainwave Cycle Fluctuations." *Science* 204: 1326-28.

Kohn, Alfie. 1993. *Punished by Rewards*. New York: Houghton-Mifflin.

Kotulak, Ronald. 1997. *Inside the Brain: Revolutionary Discoveries of How the Brain Works*. Kansas City, MO: Andrews and McMeel.

Kotulak, Ronald. April, 1993. "Unraveling Hidden Mysteries of the Brain." *Chicago Tribune*: 11-16.

Lavond, David G., Jeansok J. Kim, and Richard F. Thompson. 1993. "Mammalian Brain Substrates of Aversive Conditioning." *Annual Review of Psychology* 44: 317-42.

Mager, R. F., and J. McCann. 1963. *Learner Controlled Instruction*. Palo Alto, CA: Varian Press.

Maguire, J. 1990. *Care and Feeding of the Brain*. New York: Doubleday.

McGaugh, James. L. 1989. "Dissociating Learning and Performance: Drug and Hormone Enhancement of Memory Storage." *Brain Research Bulletin* 23: 4-5.

Nash, Madeleine. 1997. "Fertile Minds." 149 *Time* (February): 48-56.

Nicholson, Kristen. 1998. *Developing Students' Multiple Intelligences*. New York: Scholastic.

Orlock, Carol. 1993. *Inner Time*. New York: Birch Lane Press, Carol Publishing.

Phipps, Patricia A. 1997. *Multiple Intelligences in the Early Childhood Classroom*. Worthington, OH: SRA/McGraw-Hill.

Prigogine, Iyla, and Isabelle. Stengers. 1984. *Order Out of Chaos*. New York: Bantam.

Ratnesar, Romesh. 1997. "Teaching Feelings." *Time*. 150: 62.

Rechelbacher, Horst. 1987. *Rejuvenation: A Wellness Guide for Women and Men*. Rochester, VT: Thorsons Publishers.

Rose, Colin Penfield. 1997. *Accelerated Leaning into the 21st Century: The Six-Step Plan to Unlock Your Master-Mind*. New York: Doubleday.

Scartelli, Joseph P. 1984. "The Learning Brain." *Journal of Music Therapy* 21: 67-78, 341.

Scheibel, Arnold. 1994. "You Can Continuously Improve Your "Mind and Your Memory." *Bottom Line Personal* 21 (15): 9-10.

Schiller, Pam. 1997. "Brain Development Research: Support and Challenges." *Child Care Information Exchange* (September/October). Redmond, WA.

Schiller, Pam. 1998. "The Thinking Brain." *Child Care Information Exchange* (May/June). Redmond, WA.

Sirevaag, Anita M., and William T. Greenough. 1991. "Plasticity of GFAP-Immunoreactive Astrocyte Size and Number in Visual Cortex of Rats Reared in Complex Environments." *Brain Research* 540.1-2: 273-8.

Sousa, David. 1995. *How the Brain Learns*. Reston, VA: The National Association of Secondary School Principals.

Springer, Sally and Georg Deutsch. 1998. *Left Brain Right Brain*. New York: W.H. Freeman and Company.

Viadero, Debra. 1998. "Music on the Mind." *Education Week*. 25-27.

Ward, C., and Jan Jaley. 1993. *Learning to Learn*. New Zealand: A&H Print Consultants.

Webb, Douglas, and Terry Webb. 1990. *Accelerated Learning with Music: A Trainer's Manual*. Norcross, GA: Accelerated Learning Systems, 334.

Wurtman, Richard J. 1986. *Managing Your Mind and Mood through Food*. New York: Harper Collins.

Zimmerman, Barry, Sebastian Bonner, and Robert Kovach. 1996. *Developing Self-Regulatory Learners: Beyond Achievement to Self-Efficacy*. Washington, DC: American Psychological Association.

Index